Desert Sniper

How One Ordinary Brit Went to War Against ISIS

ED NASH

Little, Brown

LITTLE, BROWN

First published in Great Britain in 2018 by Little, Brown

1 3 5 7 9 10 8 6 4 2

A CIP catalogue record for this book is available from the British Library.

Hardback ISBN 978-1-4087-1133-0
C-format ISBN 978-1-4087-1134-7

Typeset in Bembo by M Rules
Printed and bound in Great Britain by
Clays Ltd, Elcograf S.p.A.

Papers used by Little, Brown are from well-managed forests and other responsible sources.

Little, Brown
An imprint of
Little, Brown Book Group
Carmelite House
50 Victoria Embankment
London EC4Y 0DZ

An Hachette UK Company
www.hachette.co.uk

www.littlebrown.co.uk

Dedicated to Jac Holmes and the Şehîd

When bad men combine, the good must associate; else they will fall one by one, an unpitied sacrifice in a contemptible struggle.

Edmund Burke,
Thoughts on the Cause of the Present Discontents

I don't want one of those goddamn politician-made wars. I want to fight in something in which human beings count.

Charles Sweeny

Contents

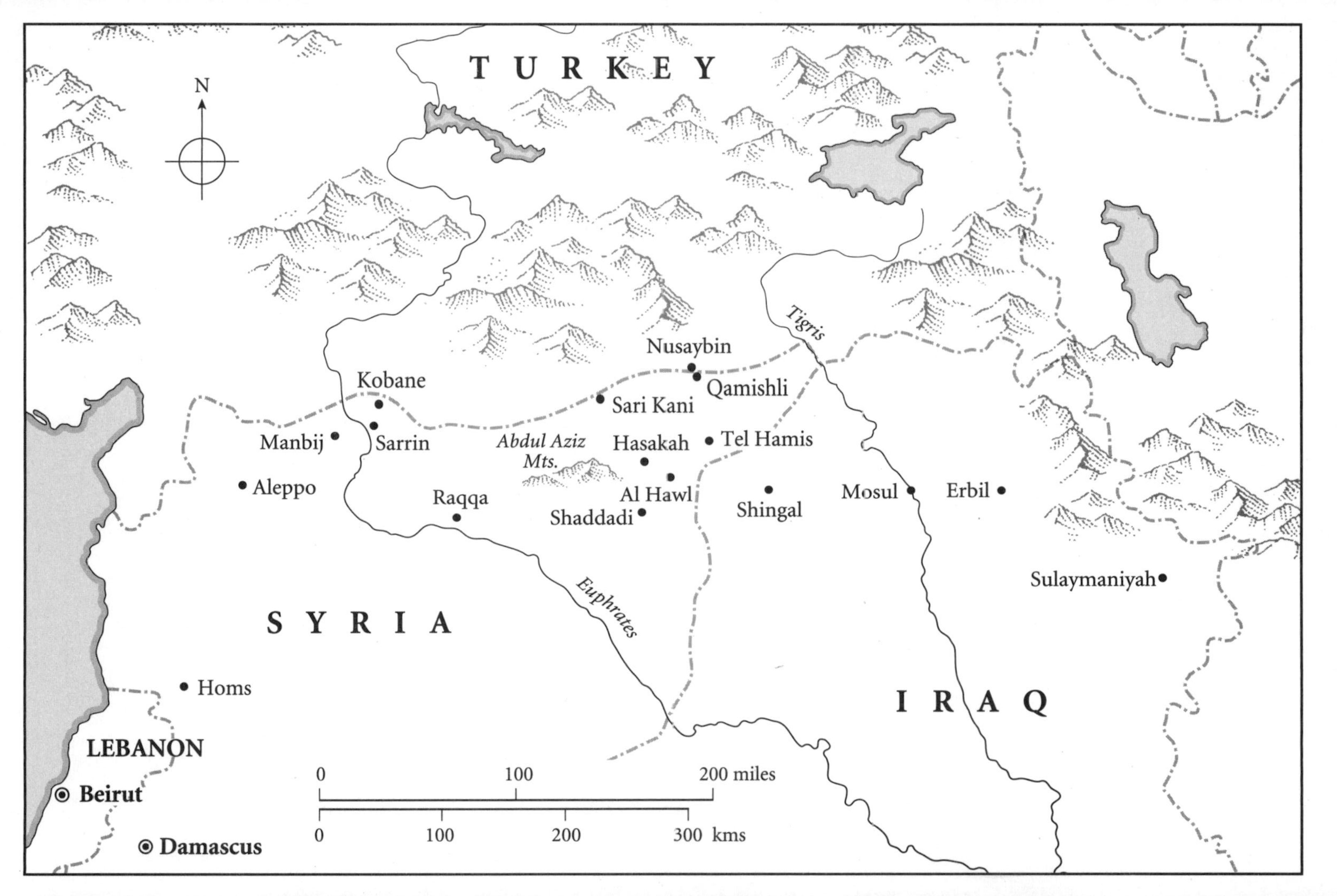
N
TURKEY
Nusaybin
Tigris
Kobane
Qamishli
Sari Kani
Manbij
Sarrin
Abdul Aziz
Mts.
Hasakah
Tel Hamis
Aleppo
Al Hawl
Raqqa
Shaddadi
Shingal
Mosul
Erbil
Sulaymaniyah
Euphrates
SYRIA
Homs
IRAQ
LEBANON
Beirut
Damascus
0
100
200 miles
0
100
200
300 kms

A Note about Names

I have not named many of the participants in this book, limiting this to foreign volunteers whom I fought or worked with closely. I have not named any of the Kurdish, Arab, Assyrian or Turkish fighters I had dealings with for two reasons. Firstly, the number of names used is fairly limited and, as a result, identification would soon be confused in the course of the narrative. Secondly, at the time of writing the situation in Syria is still in flux, and the future of those who have joined the Syrian Democratic Forces is far from clear. I have no wish to contribute to any intelligence files that may be used against them at future dates and, therefore, have not named any of these individuals. Many of these fighters, brave men and women all, are considered terrorists by certain political powers, who would happily see them dead.

In naming foreign volunteers, I have used their Kurdish *noms de guerre*, so as to protect their anonymity, although a number of them have publicly declared their service in Syria. There are two exceptions to this rule. Firstly, volunteers who were killed are a matter of public record, usually receiving a fair amount of attention in the international press. These I have referred to by their real names. Secondly, three individuals with whom I would work closely for a period of time. I will refer to them by the names Moe, Curly and Larry. They are all keen on their privacy, so I have provided them with an extra layer of anonymity. If they object to the names I have chosen, then I'm sure they will let me know.

Prologue

It was only well after the smoke and dust cloud had blown over me and settled to give me a light patina of grit that I noticed the mortar had detonated just thirty metres away. I had been sitting cross-legged on the veranda of a house on the edge of Manbij, trying to open an unripe pistachio nut, when the bomb went off. I hadn't eaten in twenty-four hours and my nails were splitting in my attempt to strip what was proving to be a stubborn opponent. A few seconds later I realised I hadn't even looked up. I'd been shelled innumerable times in the past year, and had become very good at telling where they were going to land, to the extent that my ability to judge a shell's fall was now subconscious. If you don't hear them until late, that means they are coming down on top of you.

It occurred to me that perhaps I'd been in Syria for too long, but then I managed to split the pistachio shell and my attention went back to dealing with my hunger. I popped the nut into my mouth, chewed, and then spat it out in disgust. Unripe pistachios are utterly revolting. I suppose I shouldn't have been surprised.

The dust swirled in the wind, which normally blows strongly across the flat plains and low hills of northern Syria. It is the only relief from the burning heat that bakes the ground into a rock-hard surface during the summer, but the wind freezes you to the bone in the wet winters, which transform the solid dirt into a glutinous muck that bogs down feet and vehicles. I sat and considered the houses around me, not far from the front line. I would like to say I was working towards some great revelation about the meaning of existence, or mankind, or war. But all I was really interested in was that I was away from the unrelenting fighting (mortar shells don't count), and the gnawing hunger in my belly. My mind was pleasantly blank, though I was completely aware of my surroundings. It is a strange state, a mindset of total focus that I have only found in combat.

It seems an odd situation to be in, especially as fighting in a war wasn't really on my agenda and I'd never served in the military. But in June 2015 I shouldered my rucksack and boarded the first of a series of aeroplanes that would take me to northern Syria. I would spend the best part of the next year fighting alongside the Kurdish YPG against the Islamic State – otherwise known as ISIL, ISIS or Daesh. This is the story of my experiences.

I don't intend this to be the definitive history of the war in Syria, or even of the battles I was involved in. Though I have a degree in history and have worked as a journalist, I can offer few insights into the whole sorry mess that is Syria. In combat all you are aware of is your immediate vicinity; you don't even know what is going on in a neighbouring house unless someone tells you. Trying to follow the broader complexities at a local, regional, national and international level is an impossibility. All I can tell is what I saw, what I experienced and thought. Make of it what you will.

When people find out that I fought in Syria they always ask what possessed me to travel to a war-torn country and risk my life for a cause that had nothing to do with me and that I had no need to get involved in. The answer is both complicated and very simple, and I think it holds for most foreign volunteers who travel to that country to fight.

Firstly, let me deal with the alleged motivation that gets bandied around by our detractors, and some of the press: money. We are apparently all mercenaries simply out to make a quick buck. This is absolutely not true. While certain foreign volunteers I met were definitely out there to raise their profile, to make a reputation or lay the foundations for future careers, no one did it for the money. I can safely say that it cost everyone who volunteered a considerable amount to do so and, though you would hear the occasional legends of people finding large sums of cash on dead Daesh fighters, I never met anyone who had actually known someone who had. In fact, I never even met anyone who said they knew someone *who knew someone* who found a hidden trove. It is nonsense.

Many of the foreign volunteers travelled to Syria for personal and/or political reasons. Ex-military went because they thought their talents and skills could be of use. Others went because of sympathy for the Kurds, a people with a blighted history, or because the peculiar political ideology of the YPG – a blend of anarchism, social democracy and hard-left dogma – appealed to their desire to see a different political system established that would provide an alternative to the one they had known in their home countries.

A number went because, quite frankly, they did not fit in particularly well back home. Some had family issues, some had problematic personalities, and some were even drug addicts. Some were looking for somewhere they could belong, and, for a few, the embryonic state did present just such an opportunity.

Most would be left disappointed, the reality of the situation in northern Syria being far removed from their expectations. This is hardly surprising: the place was a warzone, and still trying to establish itself as a viable entity.

I think it is fair to say that most of us – whatever our stated intentions – were driven there by a sense of adventure. After all, what more extreme experience is there than war? It's a dirty little secret that combat is the most intense thing you can engage in, and, when it's going well, there really is nothing better. Conversely, when it is going badly there is possibly nothing worse. Though we all know and hear of the horrors involved, people have always sought this thrill – and it is a thrill.

But even this, in my opinion, was not the principal reason. At the heart of why we went there was the horror inspired by Daesh. They exploded onto the international consciousness with their lightning advance across Iraq and Syria, crushing all who opposed them, including well-equipped armies. The booty they captured, both material and financial, further fuelled their expansion and, before anyone could register the reality, a fundamentalist regime was controlling a vast swath of territory and commanding an army that struck terror into their enemies. The so-called caliphate used the most brutal methods it could devise to punish those who opposed it, or otherwise did not fit with its narrow interpretation of Islam.

Tens of thousands of foreigners heeded the new regime's call to come to their territory and wage holy war against the unbelievers and apostates. There they participated in these crimes, positively revelling in them, with each fresh atrocity broadcast to the planet by Daesh's slick propaganda machine. The world watched, horrified, as entire populations were exterminated or forced to flee their homelands. Under Daesh, rape became codified, children were forced to become sex slaves, those accused of homosexuality were thrown from high buildings, and public executions for the most petty of reasons became the standard.

Allow me to spell out the sort of behaviour that Daesh used as standard on those populations, such as the Yazidis, whom ISIS decided they would not tolerate.

Armed men come to your house. If you're the man of the house, they kill you. If you are the woman, they gang rape you. The rape itself may well kill you. If not, and you're lucky, they slit your throat after they are done. If you are unlucky, they put you into one of their slave houses, where you are subject to abuse by any Daesh fighter who wants sexual gratification.

If your daughters are aged nine or above, they are old enough to be married. They are given as a reward to Daesh fighters who are considered worthy, or they are simply sold at market like cattle. They are expected to perform all wifely duties.*

* For an example of the testimony of one survivor of Daesh and their crimes, watch the evidence given by Nadia Murad Basee Taha to the United Nations Security Council on 20 December 2016.

If you have young sons (too old and they too will simply be killed) they will be indoctrinated and groomed to be future soldiers of ISIS – probably suicide bombers, as these tend to be the young and most idealistic volunteers. As part of their schooling they may well be made to murder enemies of the movement or perceived apostates, and their actions recorded and released onto the internet.

Repeat this several thousand, possibly tens of thousands, of times, and you have ISIS. So, when people ask me why I went to fight Daesh, I am, to be honest, baffled. How can any sane person not oppose such evil?

1

Making a Choice

It was in April 2015 that I made the decision to go to Syria. I was on a training run up a mountain in Karen State, Burma, with members of the Free Burma Rangers, an organisation I had been volunteering with, on and off, for the previous three years. I remember quite distinctly that I was listening to Taylor Swift's 'Shake It Off'. To my friends and old comrades who will laugh at that: I don't care – it's a great track to run to.

I try to monitor the international situation as closely as one can via the press and other open sources, and I'd been following the expansion of Daesh with some concern. It seemed obvious that, although the US Air Force had launched an intensive aerial bombing campaign the previous October, it would be some time before Daesh was destroyed.

It might seem a bit of a jump, going from assisting and training pro-democracy rebels in the jungles of Burma to fighting on the flat plains of Syria, but my motivation was the same: a desire to help people who were getting precious little aid from the outside world. Certainly, the press attention that the YPG had received during the Battle of Kobane had come to my notice, as well as a series of news articles about foreign volunteers who had gone to fight alongside the Kurds. Moreover, as the Western media's attention had waned, I thought that I might be able to use my media and information coordination skills to assist the Syrian Kurds.

This is probably a good time to explain my role at FBR, and what that organisation does. Burma is a truly beautiful country that has been blighted by more than seventy years of civil war. The Free Burma Rangers work with ethnic-minority movements throughout the country, training relief teams that go into the contested areas, providing assistance to those who need it. Generally, this means refugees who have fled to the jungles and mountains to escape the depredations of the utterly ruthless Burmese army and are forced to live in the most primitive conditions.* As a result, they are not just prey to diseases such as malaria and dengue fever, but also at risk of starvation and dysentery. In these conditions, even a cold can quickly become a lethal condition, especially among the children.

Each FBR relief team includes at least one medic who has undergone an intensive year-long training programme in treating a range of issues, from combat trauma to tropical diseases and illnesses such as pneumonia and malnutrition; both a photographer and a videographer, who document the situation, photograph Burmese army atrocities and record interviews and

* I am quite capable of going on at some length about the situation in Burma, and will do so to anyone foolish enough to ask. However, this book is not the time or place for that. Anyone interested in learning more about the issues in Burma should read anything by Bertil Lintner, who has forgotten more about this sad country than I will ever know.

testimony from victims as evidence for potential trials; and a security element, which is responsible for protecting both the team and any civilians threatened by military action.

It is important to point out that FBR's role is not primarily military, though this tends to dominate any press coverage the organisation receives: one media outlet labelled them 'like Doctors Without Borders ... with Guns'. This is both correct and inaccurate. FBR teams can, depending on the local situation, deploy armed, and that is at the discretion of the team itself, comprising volunteers from the local resistance army who best understand the level of threat, which can be considerable. In certain areas FBR teams travel as civilians, using transportation and practising medicine in towns and villages firmly under the control of the Burmese military with their tacit blessing. In other zones the mere suggestion of an FBR team in the field can lead to the army dispatching large forces in pursuits that can last for weeks as the FBR team use every trick in the guerrilla handbook to evade their hunters. In some situations, local resistance armies will send such considerable forces alongside the FBR team that they actually force the Burmese army to withdraw.

However, the FBR teams try to avoid any confrontation if at all possible. The rules of engagement drilled into the Rangers at their annual training camps are that they should only resort to arms for self-defence, or in the defence of civilians.

As part of the information department, I was responsible for collating the intelligence our field teams gathered on their patrols or from local ethnic governments, a number of which (such as the Karen and Kachin) are extremely well organised. I would then write up reports that were published by FBR and distributed to journalists, humanitarian organisations and government officials with an interest in the region. I would also act as a source for journalists requesting information on conditions in Burma, and on the political situation. In the field my job was to train the teams in what sort of information we were interested in gathering, how to fill out their patrol reports, and also other subjects such as world history and, on one memorable occasion, mathematics. Hardly my strongest subject at the best of times, my attempts to teach prospective future Shan medics, many of whom had zero (and I do mean literally *zero*) schooling, meant that even such basics as simple multiplication proved something of a forlorn hope.

It was not, and I cannot emphasise this enough, my job to fight. Nor were any of the other foreign volunteers expected to engage in combat. Every year new fresh-faced volunteers would turn up and, after receiving their basic induction speech, would ask when they were heading for the wilds and, if they were especially excitable, when they would be issued a gun. Their reaction to the answer 'You aren't likely to be sent anywhere at all dangerous and you will never be issued a gun,' would allow one to gauge how long they were likely to last. Most departed quite quickly.

However, to complicate the issue, Dave Eubank, the American founder of FBR, received considerable attention from the international press in June 2017 when a film of him charging out into Daesh fire to rescue a child, while Rangers gave him covering fire in Mosul, went viral. It is very much an organisation where you have to react to circumstance.

Logistics, human resources and information collating and report writing are not the most thrilling of occupations, but that is exactly what is required to run a programme that hopes to achieve anything of any use; anything else just descends into a bunch of yahoos running about in the jungle. And it was primarily in the office, writing reports and dealing with journalists and other advocates, that I learnt and practised the skills I thought might be of use to the Kurds in their war against Daesh.

Many of the people I speak to about my experiences want to know what sends me off to such places as Burma and Syria. Most ponder broken homes, or some deep secret that propels me to put myself at risk. They seem almost disappointed when I explain that my home life growing up was extremely stable: my parents are married and have been for forty years, I lived in the same house from the age of four, went to a good school and was a fair student, though admittedly lazy. My father worked as a warehouse manager and most of my early memories are of playing in freight yards, dodging around forklifts and under articulated lorries. No doubt today health and safety inspectors would have a stroke at children playing in such an environment, but it certainly teaches you to be aware of your surroundings.

After school I acquired a taste for travel and bounced between various jobs and touring in Asia, Africa and the UK. I went to university at the age of twenty-nine, an attempt to do *the normal thing*, and to develop some sort of plan for the future. Though I achieved a first, the attempt at normality didn't work out and so after a few years I was wandering off again. I funded myself by taking jobs I was happy to walk out on once I had saved enough money to pay for whatever it was I intended to do next. Delivery driving, removals and even a few years digging trenches and surveying sewers were some of the highlights, as well as the obligatory sales jobs.

I have never settled down and had anything remotely like a stable relationship or children. The fact is, I suppose, I am quite selfish. I like being able to head off on a whim to some remote place and not worry about a mortgage or career. Perhaps a psychologist could divine some personality trait – or flaw – that explains my attitude. My close friends have a simpler explanation. They just say, 'Oh him? He's mad.' Maybe they're correct.

I developed an interest in history while at school – and even now I am quite often to be found reading on a range of military subjects, from obscure campaigns to the latest in defence hardware – and this led me to seriously consider joining the Royal Marines when I left school.

When I told my father that I wanted to pursue a career in the military, he said:

'Well, if that's what you want to do, I understand. The only thing I ask is that you go in as an officer. At least that way you might have some say in what you do, and not just be another number.'

As my approaches to the Marines were rebuffed – the recruiting sergeant explained that at that time the corps was taking on only three officer recruits per year, and those were all university graduates of exceptional fitness – my ideas of following this career path largely fizzled out. Though I would periodically consider the option in the following years, my taste for travel also developed and I began to think that, while being a soldier was indeed an honourable profession, being at the whim of politicians who decide who and where to fight was perhaps not such a clever idea. I would say that this has led to my personal philosophy that if you are going to wage war, it is better to choose it yourself.

In fact, my motivation for going where I go and doing what I do is very simple. While I enjoy travelling and experiencing new things, I firmly believe that it is a moral duty to assist those who need aid if you are in a position to help. Why this is, I couldn't say: it seems like a cornerstone of any human society to me. Perhaps I watched too many westerns at a young age.

I am also convinced that the best way to deal with an issue is to tackle it as close to the source as possible, rather than trying to treat the symptoms of a problem. And I am a firm believer in Edmund Burke's maxim that the only thing necessary for the triumph of evil is for good men to do nothing. Without doubt I have a simplistic, somewhat inflexible view of the world, and in some ways it is pure anger at the way in which ordinary people can suffer, through no fault of their own, as they get caught in the machinations of politics and business, that sets me off on some crusade.

So it was as I panted up the mountain that I made my decision. Things in Burma had settled down, though low-level fighting in the north of the country continued. The training mission into Karen State would soon be finished, and I had largely completed a project I had been working on, highlighting the Burmese military's appointment of a well-connected lobbyist in the United States. With summer approaching, the slack period at FBR, I decided that my time might be better spent in Syria. It was relatively simple to contact the YPG and express my interest: the foreign press had made quite a meal of the early volunteers who had travelled to Syria, and publicised the contact details that were in use then, a Facebook page called the Lions of Rojava. A somewhat grandiose title, but effective, as people from across the world began to head for Rojava, the Kurdish-dominated region of northern Syria, to help in the fight.

The reaction of my fellow FBR volunteers was almost universal. When told about my intentions, they wanted to know what I intended to do in Syria and then, once they had thought about it, expressed support tinged with concern and a touch of envy. My team leader, a big, bluff ex-military policeman and football player from Ohio, summed it up in his typically succinct style:

'You're out of your goddamn mind. But if I was a bit younger I'd come with you.'

2

About the Kurds, their Factions and the YPG

Before continuing, it is probably best to explain something of the situation in which my fellow volunteers and I were miring ourselves with the Kurds and in Syria itself. The Middle East is a complex interplay of religion, race, culture and tribalism, which meant the whole region had been a powder keg for decades. Syria in 2011 had sparked and exploded, threatening the stability of the entire Middle East and causing both local and international actors to weigh in, to various degrees. The Kurds were, as always, caught right in the middle of the conflagration.

The Kurds really are a people with a tragic history. Currently classed as the largest ethnic group without their own homeland, there are an estimated forty million Kurds spread across the border regions shared by Turkey, Syria, Iraq and Iran. The Kurds themselves subdivide their scattered territory, according to which country the area is located in. Thus, Iranian Kurdistan is known as *rohilat* (east), Turkish

Kurdistan as *bakûr* (north) and Iraqi Kurdistan as *başûr* (south). *Rojava* means west.

Being the resident population of an area divided among so many countries means that the Kurds are in the classic position of a person standing in the middle of a busy crossroads: liable to get hit from any direction. The result is that the Kurds have been persecuted by every country of which they are notionally citizens. Though degrees of this persecution have tended to rise and fall depending on the whims of a particular regime, the default position in all four countries has been to suppress any hint of Kurdish nationalism or, indeed, personality. After all, Syria and Iraq are dominated by Arabs, Iran by Persians and Turkey by the Turks. None of these is particularly keen on the idea of a large section of their territory being removed from their control by what are generally considered to be a bunch of hillbillies.

This has led to multiple uprisings and the exploitation of the Kurds, both by the countries they live in, which have fanned Kurdish nationalism in their neighbours' territory when it suited their agenda, and by every external power seeking to disrupt the region for their own ends. The Kurds have been used by the British against the Turks, by Hitler to rebel against the British, by the Soviet Union against Iran and by the Americans against Saddam Hussein. This list is far from exhaustive, and none of these rebellions was successful in gaining any form of independence for the Kurds; they achieved nothing but horrendous suffering for generations and entrenched suspicion of them among the ruling ethnic majorities.

Hopes of a unified Kurdish nation are also not helped by the fact the Kurds themselves come from an immensely complex and diverse culture. There is not one Kurdish language, but seven, which use the Roman, Arabic and Persian alphabets. These in turn are subdivided into a vast array of dialects, many alien and incomprehensible to one another. Just as in their language, local Kurdish cultures and social habits also tend to be unique. In fact, it could be argued that the concept of 'being Kurdish' is something of a misnomer. The Kurds are in fact more a conglomeration of formerly remote and diverse populations who, not fitting into the mainstream ethnicities of the region, have been lumped in together.

This diversity probably helps account for the chronic factionalism that besets the Kurds' internal affairs and leads to implacable hatred among the various parties. I will not go into the full and sorry history of this because again there are better, more thorough studies. I can, however, explain some of the principal players and their influence on the Kurds of Iraq, Turkey and Syria in relation to the Syrian civil war, as well as some of the complications that this has engendered there, both for the inhabitants and the external powers.

Three Kurdish factions are the principal actors in the fight against ISIS. These are the Iraq-based political parties, the Kurdish Democratic Party (KDP) and the Patriotic Union of Kurdistan (PUK), and those who follow the political teachings of Abdullah Öcalan, who are spread across all four countries that the Kurds inhabit and enjoy some support from the Kurdish diaspora abroad. The KDP and PUK each operate their own armies, both known as the Peshmerga, and have their own zones of control in northern Iraq (also known as Kurdistan). Each detests the other and fought a civil war from 1994 to 1997, which received almost no coverage in the West.

The KDP is the political party of the Barzani family, whose forces control the south-western portion of Kurdistan, including the Syrian border region and the cities of Erbil, Hawler and Dohuk. The KDP is an autocratic, conservative and nepotistic affair, dominated by the personality of the patriarch Masoud Barzani, the notional president of the Iraqi Kurdish Region. The party tends towards a Kurdish nationalistic political bias, which is understandable as many of its key members were engaged in the long struggle for autonomy against the regime of Saddam Hussein. It is also the most commercially successful part of Iraqi Kurdistan as it sits on huge oil reserves that, when I passed through in both 2015 and 2016, were fuelling a building boom in the major cities. It is widely believed in the area that the Barzani family makes sure it gets its cut by passing laws demanding the family receives shares in any business in their part of Kurdistan.

The PUK dominates the east of northern Iraq, controlling the Iranian border, and is based in the city of Sulaymaniyah. It espouses a socialist/social democratic approach to politics. Owing to their left-wing leanings, the PUK enjoy good relations and work closely with the third party in Kurdish politics, the Kurdistan Workers Party or PKK (Partiya Karkerên Kurdistanê), generally known to its adherents as *the party.* This group is classed as a terrorist organisation by most Western nations, and is infamous for the ferocious insurgency it has fought in Turkey since 1984.

The PKK is regarded by most outside observers as a classic cold war communist party that is trying to establish an independent Kurdish state in Turkey, which will be shaped as a workers' paradise on the model of Marxism-Leninism. A relic of the party's origins in this doctrine (other than being referred to as *the party*) is the way members refer to each other as *heval*, which translates literally as friend, but a more accurate translation in terms of intent would be comrade.

However, to regard the PKK as a Marxist leftover is a simplification, and mistaken. The complexities of the organisation's ideology are one of the factors that make supporting the Kurds in Syria, and the legal status of volunteers who join them, problematic.

The PKK is part of a much broader coalition of parties – which include the party that represents the Syrian Kurds, the PYD (Partiya Yekîta Demokrat, or Democratic Union Party) – that subscribe to the ideological, philosophical and historical writings of Abdullah Öcalan, a Kurdish political theorist and guerrilla leader affectionately nicknamed Apo (*uncle* – presumably the root of the name Apogee, by which his adherents are generally referred to) who founded and led the movement, and subsequently developed the idea of democratic confederalism, also known as Apoism, as his ideal method of government while in jail in Turkey – where, at the time of writing in early 2017, he remains, as far as anyone knows. This political theory is a gelling of Marxism-Leninism, Stalinism, anarchism and libertarian ideals. Broadly speaking, it espouses the idea that central government should be kept to a minimum, that power should be highly decentralised and local issues resolved at a local level, not to mention that regional/racial/religious customs should be respected, along with the need for gender equality. It also stands for a fairer redistribution of wealth along similar lines to European social democracy.

This broad array of inputs means that, depending on whom you talk to, there is a wide range of opinions available about what the Apogees hope to achieve, a good example being whether or not the Kurds should have their own country. The ideology sees itself as a means of destroying the corrosive nationalism that pervades so much of the current world system, and loudly proclaims the fact. Under democratic confederalism, there would be no need for nation states or borders; all creeds would be respected and issues would be dealt with by democratic consensus. Thus establishing a country called Kurdistan within the international order is not only not on their agenda, but actually anathema, given what they stand for. However, among the rank and file, talk of establishing a country the Kurds can call their own is extremely common. So what is the true position? After a year living with Kurds I still don't know, although I suspect their political leadership, like politicians everywhere, will react to circumstance to suit their own aims.

Technically speaking, there are a number of elements in the ideology that would, in my opinion, be of real benefit to the region. The emphasis on equality and non-interference in personal beliefs is definitely an improvement on many of the existing social structures in the Middle East, especially those of the more conservative Arab areas. It also stands in stark contrast to the intolerance of Daesh. In reality, of course, the application of democratic confederalism is not as clear-cut as its practitioners and advocates in the wider world make out, but then no political system is ever the utopia it is intended to be.

Most of Öcalan's followers regard him with what can only be described as religious adulation. His face is plastered across walls and his writings are regarded with a veneration comparable to religious fundamentalism. The irony is that Öcalan has written against the cult of the personality, but still this state of affairs persisted while I was in Syria. Many of the foreign volunteers would refer to the ever-present pictures of Apo ironically as 'moustached Jesus', such is the adoration in which he is held. Indeed, I have heard at least one Kurd openly state that for those who subscribe to his ideals, Öcalan is their equivalent.

There are some bizarre quirks thrown up by democratic confederalism. Coca-Cola is considered capitalist and not widely available, though that situation had changed slightly by the time I left Rojava in July 2016. However, Pepsi is *boş* (good). Why, I have no idea, but I suspect it could be simply that Apo once said he preferred Pepsi – this is literally the most sensible answer I can come up with. Similarly, iPhones are evil, but Samsung is fine, and if you want to use the internet it is automatically assumed that you want to use Facebook, as many Kurds have limited educations and are unable to access many websites that are in foreign languages as a result. You are sternly told that Facebook is *no boş* and capitalist, and then taken aside and asked to friend the person giving you the warning.

There appears to be a knee-jerk reaction to certain forms of modernity among the leadership, which naturally means everything proscribed is of fascination to the rank and file. The prohibition of internet communications makes some sense in that the Kurds are paranoid about security and many firmly believe that the whole organisation is riddled with Turkish spies. An example of this concerns the issuing of the *nobat* list, the guard roster that is set every night. It is against the rules both to try to find out when your duty hour is, and to tell someone else when theirs will be. This situation makes most Western volunteers extremely irritable, as it is nice to know if and when you are liable to be kicked awake in the middle of the night. But the prohibition exists (though it is often broken) to prevent any agent within the organisation alerting enemies as to when they can safely attack.

The fanaticism with which the ideology is embraced does, somewhat ironically, remind me of the same steadfast dedication displayed by Islamic fundamentalists. In many ways, Öcalan's ideas have simply replaced Islam as the primary belief system in the areas where he holds sway. Certainly, elements seem similar, particularly the emphasis on *Şehîd* – martyrs. Posters of the fallen can be seen everywhere and reports of those who have died fighting are in the news every night on the Kurdish television channels.

Additionally, the Apogees practise a form of criticism/self-criticism known as *tac mil*. These solemn sessions combine a debriefing with a chance for unit members to air their grievances. They are used by everyone, from the smallest three- or four-person fire team right up to a mass meeting where troops get the chance to criticise the performance of the generals who commanded a particular operation. However, the sheer seriousness of a tac mil makes it almost a religious occasion; I've seen senior commanders go from making brusque demands for attention to retreating and sitting quietly and patiently until the meeting is over once they've realised that a tac mil is taking place. I can only compare it to intruding on a sacred ritual. Indeed, the only time I have known a tac mil break up without its business complete was when Daesh managed to drop a Katyusha rocket onto the building in which we were holding the meeting. But more on that later.

The Yekîneyên Parastina Gel (YPG), the force that I and the majority of other foreign volunteers joined, translates as 'People's Protection Units' and is, in effect, a militia. The Apogee theory of decentralisation means that, ideally, each village, town and district would raise its own militia, and these would combine and coordinate against any external threat. The idea is that by diversifying military power no single racial, religious or political group can dominate. Broadly speaking, it is probably not unfair to compare the YPG to the minutemen of the American War of Independence, although they are, as I have pointed out, part of a broader social philosophy.

For outside parties this is a delicate issue that has led to great divisions; these have, in turn, caused huge complications in the war against Daesh and other extremist groups. The Turks naturally regard the YPG and any other group subscribing to Öcalan's theories as one and the same and, as such, see the development of any sort of independent structure with an Apogee element on their border as an intolerable threat to their security. The growth of the YPG in Syria and its successful expulsion of Al Nusra, the Syrian wing of Al Qaeda, from Rojava in 2013, meant that the Turks suddenly went from facing an insurgency in their remote regions by a group with scant outside support, to the possibility of insurgents having a safe region where they could recruit, train and equip substantial forces. This led to the Turks taking active military action against the Kurds in northern Syria and even, it is alleged, supplying aid to groups fighting them in Syria.*

Naturally, fear on the part of Turks has meant a great many problems have arisen with its NATO allies, especially when America waded into the war in northern Syria, followed shortly after by a number of other Western nations. At this moment, the YPG went from being merely an unimportant militia to a force much praised in the media as the outside world's best weapon in the war against ISIS. The Turks insist that their allies not sponsor or equip the YPG – who are, to them, terrorists – while the West, and particularly the United States, declares the PKK are terrorists and they see no connection between the two organisations.

Fighting alongside the YPG is the Yekîneyên Parastina Jin (YPJ) – the Women's Protection Unit. This militia follows the ideological outline set out by Öcalan and is designed to spearhead the movement's ideas on equality. Most units are heterogeneous and men and women train and fight together. As Kurdish society is strongly patriarchal, the YPJ really is a remarkable development. However, there are strict rules of behaviour and, though comradeship between members of both sexes is fostered, if a man and a woman are judged to be too close to one another they are subject to formal criticism and possible retribution. Sexual relations are severely punished and, as many members dedicate their lives to the organisation,

* A great example is when Turkish gendarmes seized trucks loaded with weapons – allegedly bound for ISIS – only to have Turkish intelligence, who were escorting the materiel, threaten them: Humeyra Pamuk and Nick Tattersall, 'Exclusive: Turkish intelligence helped ship arms to Syrian Islamist rebel areas', Reuters, 21 May 2015.

they are abandoning the possibility of ever having children. As this commitment is normally made when in their teens, it can become a source of friction as a fighter ages and grows tired of war. In my comparatively brief time in Syria there were a number of scandals in which senior personnel either deserted to start families elsewhere, or just said 'enough' and refused to serve any more, as they felt that they had done more than their fair share.

In terms of its organisation, the YPG is split into a regional brigade structure, normally created at the canton or major-city level. These brigades are responsible for defending their territory and, when advancing against ISIS, for forming the army that will attack. They are assisted in this by the Mobile Brigade, which is in effect the teeth of the army and sent wherever it is needed. The Mobile Brigade sees more action and is composed of more experienced soldiers; it is to this brigade that many foreigners come, as they are more likely to be involved in major offensive operations against Daesh.

Each brigade is composed of a number of tabors, a unit broadly equivalent to a platoon and made up of between ten and a hundred personnel. Tabors are generally infantry units, but each brigade also has specialist tabors composed of heavy weapons, which includes tanks, mortars, armoured personnel carriers (APCs), panzers – home-built armoured vehicles – and dushkas, which are generally known in the West as technicals. Dushkas are usually a pick-up truck (normally a Toyota Hilux or Land Cruiser) with a heavy weapon mounted on the back, normally a single- or twin-barrel weapon of 12.7mm, 14.5mm or 23mm calibre. These play the part of field guns and artillery support as the YPG has no artillery that I am aware of (apart from a few rocket launchers – more on those later), and are for laying down heavy fire. Brigades also have a sniper and a sabotage tabor: the first provides marksmen to other units as required and the latter is a bomb-disposal/demolition unit with a commando role. Sabotage units are responsible for clearing Daesh booby traps and mines, then reusing them behind ISIS lines against their former owners.

The tabors themselves are in effect semi-independent war bands. Though they are completely reliant on the YPG for supplies, each unit is very much dominated by the personality of its commander. Because of the anti-military bias of the organisation, fighters have the ability to move between units. Thus, an unsuccessful or unpopular commander can soon find himself facing an evaporation of his manpower as his troops request transfers to units with commanders who they trust more, or who will allow them to see a greater share of the action. Tabor commanders who suffer heavy casualties will find both their own troops leaving and sanctions being imposed by higher command, including removal from their post and even prison if they are judged to be especially negligent.

3

Arriving in Iraq, Terrifying Transportation and Learning the YPG Way of War

June/July 2015

Decision made to go, it was simply a matter of boarding a flight in Bangkok and heading for Sulaymaniyah via a connecting flight in Turkey. Despite the wars raging in the south between the Peshmergas, the Iraqi army and Daesh, northern Iraq showed no real signs of the conflict. Having said that, getting off the plane it occurred to me that I might possibly be walking into a trap. Daesh, after all, had the nasty habit of cutting the heads off foreigners they got their hands on, and though I was confident things would work out, all I'd actually had was contact with an unknown person through a Facebook page and a phone number for someone that I was to get the cab driver to call to receive directions.

I was reassured by the reactions of the Kurdish customs

officials. They were rigorously scanning all arrivals' passports and asking aggressive questions in what was either Kurdish or Arabic. But as soon as I handed over my British passport, the official looked at me, said 'Thank you for coming,' and stamped me through. I was surprised by this, although with hindsight I realise that Western men (and some women) travelling light, alone and looking nervous, were a common occurrence; these officials knew exactly why we had come and were grateful for our efforts. While the politics of the Kurds might have been fractious in the extreme, to the average person the fact that we foreigners had come to fight and possibly die for them, their kin and Kurds generally meant that we received respect. That Sulaymaniyah is firmly in the hands of the PUK also meant we were safe, though I did not realise this until later.

Outside the airport I gave the contact number to a cab driver, who, after ringing, received directions to a hotel in the bustling city. As we pulled up my nerves were jangling, I'll admit, because this was the moment where I would find out if I was about to get issued an orange jumpsuit and soon become acquainted with the wrong end of a gutting knife. The contact greeted me and took me up to a room where, to my great relief, I met some fellow volunteers waiting to go into Syria. There were four of us: two Americans, one Canadian and me.

A couple of days later we were taken to a camp in the mountains near the border, enduring both a terrifying taxi ride to get there (which in all seriousness was one of the most dangerous things I endured in all the time I was involved in the war) and the suspicious glances of guards as we passed the checkpoints dotted throughout their territory. At the camp we settled in and started learning the Kurdish customs and language that we would need for our time in Rojava. I discovered that shorts were an absolute no-no after going for a run and coming back to find the woman commander at the camp regarding me with outright horror. Long trousers were obligatory, as were long sleeves, around YPJ. It was also here that I was given my Kurdish *nom de guerre* – Botan, which is a mountain in the Kurdish region of Turkey.*

I waited at the mountain camp as more volunteers drifted in to make up a group to be smuggled across. This took a couple of weeks and as new volunteers arrived, veterans were passing through and heading home. This was an important opportunity to get information about the situation and what we were getting into from guys who had been there. It was here that we learned of the bounty that ISIS was supposed to have put on every foreign volunteer – prompting me to joke about how I could hand the lot of them in and retire a wealthy man, and leading to joshing about the actual respective value we would place on each other, normally in measurements of goats – and how we would be well advised to keep a bullet in our pockets for ourselves, or else a Daesh 'suicide grenade', if we came across one, that would detonate instantly. Taking your own life would be vastly preferable to capture by Daesh. It was plain that things were going to be rough when Şêr (lion) staggered into the camp. He was a Brit

* The YPG use a naming system to protect the identities of their members. Most of these are taken from specific areas that are of historical importance to the Kurds, meteorological conditions (*birûsk* – lightning – is a popular example), or words associated with revolution, such *berxwedan* – struggle.

who had served in a sabotage tabor, and had been hit in the neck and jaw when a mine had been triggered. The explosion injured a number of volunteers and killed one young Australian, Reece Harding. The Kurds had limited medical resources and Şêr was in a bad way, with an infection setting in. Fortunately one of the volunteers had medical training and cleaned the wound as best he could. Şêr returned to the UK, and after a brief recovery period came back to his beloved sabotage unit.

At the end of June my turn came. We crossed over the border and were taken to the 'foreigners' academy', where we signed an agreement that we would serve at least six months in Syria with the YPG in return for our airfares home being paid, would try to learn Kurdish and undertake basic military exercises, and were issued YPG uniforms. We were, at the time, the largest group of volunteers to join the organisation. The so-called training lasted two weeks; we were given Kalashnikovs with no bolts to practise drill and conduct nightly guard duties. We got to fire a grand total of six rounds from the AK and three from a PKM machine gun. We were also allowed to practise throwing rocks at a tyre, to mimic the use of grenades, and were shown an RPG. Literally, a Kurd held up a launcher tube and said, 'This is an RPG.' The Dragunov rifle, the principal sniper weapon of the YPG, was broken before the demonstration and I did not even get to look at it; ironic, as this weapon would be the one I used the most during my time in Syria.

Even at this early stage I and the other volunteers could see problems with how the YPG viewed itself and its ethos. The Kurds were very proud of what had been achieved since its foundation in 2011. They had, in their eyes, seen off Al Nusra with only a handful of small arms and civilian weapons, intimidated the Assad regime into all but accepting their hegemony in northern Syria, and been the only force across the Middle East to have defeated ISIS. There was some truth in this, but not to the wildly optimistic levels that the Kurds seemed to have.

'We fight as guerrillas. Guerrillas always beat soldiers as they have belief. Our tactics are guerrilla tactics and so we cannot be beaten.' This is what we were repeatedly told.

The truth was that the basic squad-level techniques the YPG used, certainly at this time, were awful. Some units, usually ones that had seen a lot of fighting, were of better quality. But the belief that hit-and-run attacks would be successful was badly mistaken. I believe this had been identified by the higher echelons, who realised that the need to go on the offensive and hold ground would require a different approach. But this appreciation was going to take a long time to get down to the squad level.

Needless to say, the foreign veterans, many of whom had combat experience from Iraq and Afghanistan, were appalled by the level of training and did their best to conduct their own lessons within the group, to teach things like clearing houses and basic combat manoeuvres. The best of these was a first aid lesson given by an ex-Norwegian army medic, who ran us through simple things such as how to check a casualty thoroughly and apply dressings and tourniquets. The veterans passing out had warned us that IEDs and mines would be a major cause of injuries, and that tourniquets would prove to be critical, especially as the Kurds seemed to have zero first aid capability and were losing countless injured soldiers for want of the most urgent basic treatment.

It was in this period that I met a Kurd named Renas, who worked for the YPG's media department and it seemed, on the face of it, a match made in heaven. When he found out what work I had been involved in prior to coming to Syria, he practically clapped his hands. The war had taken a heavy toll on personnel and he was snowed under trying to run the department and his own projects. My offer to act as a press contact for external journalists matched his need perfectly, and he told me that once my time at the academy was done I should request to work with him at the nearby base of Karatchok. As this was what I had come to Syria expecting to do, things seemed to be working out perfectly. More fool me.

4

Going to War – Kobane and Sarrin

July/August 2015

After two weeks, our time at the academy finished and the commander of the district came to us and asked where we wanted to serve. I said that I had expected to work at Karatchok with the YPG media department, and that Renas was waiting for me to join him. The commander looked blank, then told me he would have to talk to Renas and that, until then, I might as well stay with the other foreigners, who to a man had asked to go to combat units at the front. Fighting was raging in the city of Sarrin in Kobane Canton, so we were all going there.

We were taken up the hill to Karatchok and issued our weapons, webbing, magazines and ammunition. The rifles were all old Kalashnikovs from various countries that had seen their fair share of hard use. Mine was an old Iraqi model that, though it was so old the blueing was coming off the steel, never missed a beat. And with that we were crammed into a small van and set off for Kobane.

The trip was tense, to say the least. There were fourteen of us all packed into the back of a Mercedes Vito, which was not conducive to comfortable travel. We were aware that we were heading into a warzone with a population whose reliability and allegiances we had no real knowledge of. If we were hit by an ambush, there was no way we could protect ourselves or even exit the vehicle which was, quite frankly, like a clown car, with bulky Westerners all sitting on each other, their weapons and their grenades. This predicament was made worse when, after several hours on the road, we came to a sudden halt. A truck bomb had blown up on the road a half hour before and everything had been stopped while the Asayish, the paramilitary police, dealt with the situation. Needless to say, for all of us crammed into the baking, static vehicle like sardines, this was not a happy predicament. We were a dream target and we knew it. Fortunately, the driver was no happier than we were, and drove off the road and jumped the long queue. The Asayish who flagged him down got a surprise when he stopped the vehicle, only to find it full of heavily armed foreigners. Realising that our presence would soon get around, and that this could turn the whole area into a shooting gallery, he wisely moved us on sharply.

I wasn't too sure what to expect from Kobane. Obviously, we knew that a savage battle had been fought there only a few months before, a battle that marked the turnaround in the war with ISIS, and their long retreat; but Daesh was still not done with the place. A couple of weeks earlier, while we had been waiting in the mountains, their forces had launched a series of suicide attacks on the city, which had killed hundreds, including over one hundred children in a school, over two days. We knew that we were going to a place that had suffered horribly and was liable to be targeted again. But what we found touched us all profoundly.

Much of the city was utterly devastated. What the months of house-to-house fighting had not destroyed, the Americans had finished. Every street was damaged and 70 per cent of the city had been levelled. The buildings in these areas were gutted concrete shells. And people were still living among the ruins. That was the real miracle of Kobane. Not only were people still living there, the place was thriving. Shops were open, children played in the street and people went about their business. There was a sense of triumph in the air. Kobane had been taken to the brink and survived. More than that, the people recognised that their city was now a rallying point, a place where history had been made. It was the place where the tide had turned against a great evil. And they were jubilant – even as they picked their way through the rubble.

And, what is more, we were rock stars. To suddenly have fourteen foreigners turn up in YPG uniform wandering the streets literally caused traffic to stop, especially as one of us, Pilling, stood almost seven feet in his boots. I can only compare it to being Allied soldiers during the liberation of Europe. Everywhere we went people stopped us to shake our hands, invite us in for food or tea and thank us for coming. The fact that we had come from all over the world to help them in their darkest hour was a source of inspiration for us as much as for them. It gave us an appreciation of the people that we had come to fight for.

There were more sombre things to see, though. We visited

the school where the children and their teachers had been massacred, and along with every accepted offer of tea from insistent and beaming hosts would come a thoughtful and pained mention of those lost in the siege. Everyone had friends and/or family who had been killed by Daesh, and the sheer disgust for the movement and its followers was palpable. It made us all thoroughly convinced that we had been right to come.

After a few days in Kobane our orders came through. Two of the guys stayed to help in the hospitals and with the ambulances that served the front line. The rest of us were split into two groups; half were sent to front-line positions on the Euphrates to guard the river from any attempt by Daesh to cross while the rest of us went thirty miles south to Sarrin, where the battle to take the town was coming to an end. Six of us were packed into the back of another van and dispatched to join a unit that was holding a school. The schools, indeed all public buildings in Syria, are built to a similar pattern and are obviously designed to act as strongpoints in the event of civil disturbance. They all have high, thick walls around their perimeters, sturdy gates and overlook neighbouring buildings, creating excellent fire positions from behind concrete parapet walls. This one was no exception, but it also demonstrated that any defensive structure is only strong if adequately manned and defended. A few days before our arrival the school had been overrun in a surprise attack. As it had been well behind the lines, in what was thought to be a secure area, it had only been garrisoned by three or four YPG. The evidence of the desperate fight they must have made, and their end, was all too plain to see. Spent cases littered the courtyard and the roof, and blood smears showed where their bodies had been dragged out onto the playground and then burnt. The corpses had been removed, but the cracked and stinking flagstones told their grim story all too well.

There was other evidence of how savage the fighting had been in this 'secure' area. Our arrival was warmly greeted by the tabor we had been assigned to. They had been forced to man the school more heavily after the surprise attack and so six fresh bodies meant they could leave us with a fire team and get back into the main fight. The troops left behind briefed us on what had happened and how recent events had shown that nowhere in Sarrin could be considered secure.

'Just before you arrived we were attacked by many suicide bombers, maybe twenty,' the team commander told me.

'Oh, yes?' I said. 'How close did they get?'

He waved an arm languidly at the horizon.

'See all the dogs?' he asked.

In a ring extending about two hundred metres around us, little clusters of dogs were busily picking through the dismembered parts of the would-be martyrs. They had been shot – and detonated – before they could get close enough to do any damage. They don't put that in the suicide-bomber recruitment brochures.

My little squad settled in at the school, which we nicknamed the Alamo, in reference to both its appearance and the fate of its previous defenders, and our days revolved around doing two shifts of guard duty and feeding the fleas that infested our blankets. We were warned that ISIS cells were still very much a threat, to the extent that every night we barricaded ourselves in, and every morning we would do a full combat sweep of the perimeter before even using the toilet, in case infiltrators had got in and laid mines. The weather was searingly hot and, even though I had an advantage in having come from the tropics to Syria, it was still a big step up in temperature. The wind provided scant relief as it was hot and full of sand, as well as scented with death and decomposition from all the bodies bloating out there in the sun. I was fortunate to have good guys in my team as the heat, monotony, bad food and persistent parasites could have led to major issues. The squad consisted of one other Brit, Soro, a former infantryman and veteran of Afghanistan; Del Gesh, another Afghan vet, from the Canadian Army; and three Americans – Barran, who was meant to be making a documentary with a Kurdish film crew, but they had, in the usual chaos of Rojava, been delayed; the giant Pilling; and, finally, Kemal from Georgia, who I'd nicknamed Inbred in honour of his home state. This nickname became known throughout Rojava, and even after the war, interviews he gave were occasionally attributed to Inbred. This will probably be my greatest contribution to history.

Sarrin was to prove the classic war cliché: hours of boredom, combined with a few remarkable incidents. Although the fighting was largely over and the town seemed devoid of any human life apart from Kurdish troops, jets rumbled continually overhead, interspersed with the whine of Predator drones. Airstrikes exploded regularly in the distance, combined with the noise of ISIS booby traps and the *pop-boom* of dushkas as our colleagues chased the last of Daesh out into the hinterland, or back across the Euphrates only a few kilometres distant. Sometimes the airstrikes would be so intense they sounded like firecrackers being set off.

One night a shot woke us from our sound sleep. Kemal, who'd been on guard, was crouching down behind the parapet.

'Err . . . I think someone just shot at me,' he said.

It was the first of many bullets that would spin past my friend's head as he spent well over a year in the country and saw some of the heaviest fighting of any foreign volunteer.

We spent the days wandering the deserted streets, mainly looking for houses that still had water in their tanks so that we could shower, but also to stave off the crushing boredom. Despite the town being abandoned, we always travelled in at least pairs and fully armed. The outskirts of Sarrin, where we were based, were a rabbit warren, and getting lost was a risk. But there were some landmarks we could use to navigate, the most obvious being a dismembered suicide bomber lying in a narrow lane between rows of houses that was on the main route we used. His limbs and torso were scattered around, rotting, while his head lay, mouth agape, with the look of surprise that death can give. It may sound horrible, and I suppose it was, but you soon adapt to such things and Dead Daesh Corner soon became a recognised direction for getting somewhere.

One night something so remarkable happened that few people believe me when I tell them. I was pulling my guard shift, the moon was full and I was watching the berm, a ditch with the spoil thrown up behind it to form a rough barricade, that had been built to protect us from any suicide vehicles launched against us. I was in a semi-blissful state, enjoying the cool breeze that contrasted wonderfully with the baking heat of the day, when something caught my eye and set off some primal instinct in my brain. A low figure, moving with incredible stealth, was creeping along the edge of the berm. Even though the moon was quite brilliant, bathing the whole area in a sharp light, I couldn't make out what it was. I was used to dogs wandering around in the night; with the human population gone they had become feral and were in the habit of picking over any body parts or corpses lying around. But this moved like no dog. The hair actually stood up on my neck, something I'd rarely experienced before, and I slowly moved my rifle to my shoulder, flicked off the safety and sighted on the mysterious snooper.

One of the Kurds came over to me and, with a whisper, said I should lower my weapon and handed me the thermal sight that he had been using to watch the other side of the town. There, staring straight at me without a care, only twenty metres away, was a leopard. I've been to Africa and Asia many times, gone on safaris, hiked for months at a time in places where these animals can be found in large numbers and never caught so much as a whiff of one. And here, in a town in the middle of a warzone, one was staring at me quite unconcerned. I was astonished.

The leopard regarded me for a few moments, making me glad of my high perch, before turning and slinking off further into the town and out of sight. I could follow his progress by the alarmed barking of dogs as he passed through their territory. The Kurd took his scope back and grinned.

'Daesh dinner,' he said, and went back to his position.

Despite the fighting now being well away from our location we still got to witness the terrible consequences of the war. The 31st of July, a Friday, was quiet until after the evening prayers. Then, we were put on alert. A large group of civilians were approaching, trying to get away from the fighting. As Daesh loved to put suicide bombers in such crowds, it all got very tense as we hurriedly positioned ourselves to face an all-round assault. The few Kurds with us were extremely nervous. With hindsight, it was the presence of so many foreigners in one place that had them twitching – we were without doubt the prime target for any assault, as Daesh would be able to make great capital from our deaths after their run of defeats since Kobane.

Fortunately, the refugees were just that, so the YPG made arrangements for their housing for the fast approaching night and evacuation back to Kobane in the morning. For duty guard, I was sent to cover the road at the front of the school, where I could also help keep an eye on our visitors. While doing this, another car pulled up and we suddenly had a crisis to deal with.

A man had stepped on a mine while attempting to get to the evacuation point with his children. He had massive lower-leg damage and the kids had extensive shrapnel wounds. I took one look at them and knew that without immediate treatment they were not going to make it. The Kurds' ability to administer first aid was at that time completely non-existent, none of the troops had any real training in how to deal with combat trauma and first-line treatment was entirely in the hands of a few ambulances that could do little more than apply a dressing and give an injection of morphine, if they had it. The supply situation was precarious and pharmaceutical supplies were extremely limited.

That said, we did have our personal first aid kits, and I knew that Soro had combat first aid training and had treated child IED victims in Afghanistan. It was time to take action.

'I get Soro,' I told the Kurds in my poor Kurdish. 'He is war doctor.'

And so began what was quite literally a running row with the YPG as I hurried back across the playground yelling for Soro to grab his gear and get out front. The Kurds were worried about us all coming out of our fortress into the open, especially as they were concerned that there might be a potential attacker among the refugees.

The little girl was four or five, the boy perhaps three. He was terribly injured and weakly crying out for his mother, too badly hurt to scream. His sister was catatonic, with large open wounds to her feet and a serious head injury. Their father, a man with more courage than I could ever muster, was only concerned for his kids, ignoring the hideous wounds to his leg, which was now just a length of bone that had been flensed by the blast. Soro applied our one proper tourniquet to his mangled leg and then turned his attention to the boy. The ambulance had arrived, and this set off another set of problems. The ambulance was the medical facility for the entire zone – one stretcher, some saline and a couple of syringes of morphine (only one of which we were allowed to use), but not even proper field dressings. The operators were trained to give injections and that was it. In spite of these limitations, the medic (so-called) was extremely resentful to have other people trespassing on what he saw as his turf.

Trying to figure out the extent of the boy's injuries, Soro asked for water to clean away the blood so he could assess the damage. He was curtly told there was no water, so, in desperation, he grabbed a bottle of medical alcohol and swabs to do the job instead. This started an almighty row as the ambulance medic began shouting that it was only for cleaning hands. I was quite glad that Soro had left his rifle outside the vehicle, and I think that violence would have shortly followed if one of the senior Kurds, who had a better knowledge of Soro and understanding of his capabilities and training, hadn't told the guy to back off.

While Soro worked on the boy I tried to help his sister. She was fading in and out of consciousness, not talking. I cleaned the gash on her head as best I could, then, unable to do anything else, I took her hand and talked to her. Her little fist grasped onto my finger with a weak grip, but at least she was responding.

'How's she doing?' Soro asked over his shoulder.

'Not good, but she's holding onto me, so she's still here,' I replied.

'Get to her soon as I can,' he said. Then the little boy turned his head and vomited blood all over the floor.

'Oh Christ! They need hospital ASAP!'

The ambulance couldn't even transport them, as it was needed in Sarrin in case anything else happened. A civilian car had been called, and the children and their father would be taken in that on the hour-long drive to Kobane. The hospital there was basic, little more than a large doctor's surgery by Western standards, but it was all there was. It is no small thing getting a man whose leg is being held on by shattered bone, scraps of flesh and bandages, into the back seat of a car. Getting two severely hurt children in as well complicated things further. But with enough bodies lifting them in as carefully as possible, we managed it and the car sped away into the dark, lights off so as not to present a target.

I was never able to find out what happened to them, or even if they survived.

Guard duty still had to be mounted, but we were all pretty wired by what had just happened.

'How the fuck can we have millions of dollars of bombs and missiles being dropped on demand all over the fucking place, but we can't even get fucking bandages or painkillers?' fumed Soro.

He was right, and our experience gave us something of a purpose. The terrible medical situation meant that the former soldiers in our outfit were the best-trained medics in the warzone. It was by now obvious that the Kurds were intent on keeping us out of the firing line until they were sure of our capabilities. This was completely reasonable, to be fair. There had been a number of 'Rambo' types who had passed through Rojava, and had proved to be idiots. The Kurds had naturally become suspicious of any claims of expertise made by foreigners. Fortunately the events of that night had raised our standing in this regard, so the next morning we suggested that we set the school up as a casualty clearing post. It was a logical solution. Casualties could be triaged at the Alamo, which was well-defended, somewhere our medics could work to stabilise them before onward transport to Kobane. We'd been warned by those leaving about how dire the situation was in terms of front-line treatment and how so many died from simple things like a lack of tourniquets. Here was somewhere we could make a difference.

We explained our intentions to the rest of our unit, and

they conceded, cautiously, that it was a good idea. A morning's scavenging threw up straps and steel rods that we were able to fashion into impromptu tourniquets, and a large metal work-bench with holes drilled through it, which would have provided an excellent treatment table. Unfortunately, our efforts came too late as the next day we were told that the campaign was finished and the last pockets of Daesh had been routed. There was no need for our aid post and we were now well and truly surplus to requirements. Luckily, at this moment, Barran's errant film crew finally ran us to ground. They'd been delayed getting across the border and now wanted Barran to come with them to make a documentary about the war and the foreign volunteers. This left us all to make our choices. Other volunteers had advised us to spend some time with our initial Kurdish unit to learn more of the language and culture before seeking to move to any of the Mobile Brigade units. This would establish our reputation with the YPG and, in turn, assist our transfer requests when we made them. But the chance to leave what was now a quiet zone was too much for many of the lads, and they opted to go with Barran to greener pastures and try their luck with other units. I was sad to see them go, but understood. We'd all come here to do something, and sitting around in Sarrin was not going to provide any action. Del Gesh and I opted to stay with our tabor and said farewell to our friends.

Our decision sat well with our Kurdish colleagues, who no doubt found it far easier to deal with two ignorant foreigners than with six, and we were moved to a rather nice house overlooking an inlet that fed into the Euphrates. As the river banks were formed by high hills, the inlet offered Daesh forces an obvious place to try to make landings, either for scouting, raiding or a major assault. We set to fortifying our position and making sure our machine gun and RPG each had a good position to shoot at any assault attempt. The other side of the river was full of Daesh and they stayed there largely unmolested. Coalition airstrikes had pretty much dried up after the liberation of Sarrin, and they were in any case limited to military targets. Without ground direction, which they were not receiving here, they could not strike the streams of traffic running along the roads that traced the other side of the river because they could not be sure it was not civilian. We had no weapons with enough range to reach across the wide river, so we settled into what was a much more comfortable location than the school. The Kurds in our unit had been fighting hard for months, even years, and were more than happy to set up home. The area was devoid of human beings and we soon found a host of animals migrating to our location, looking for food, water and protection from the packs of dogs that were becoming feral. Within days we had been joined by numerous cats, geese, ducks, chickens and even a donkey and her foal. We spent the following days keeping a languid watch on the river, performing basic agricultural work gathering the ripening fruit and vegetables from the abandoned farms and gardens nearby and also getting the water pumps running to make sure our produce continued to flourish. It was, quite frankly, an idyllic place for a holiday.

This time with the Kurds also demonstrated how superstitious they could be, despite the drilling they receive on discarding such beliefs. As it was the height of summer and scorching hot, one day we took the opportunity to have a swim in the Euphrates. Five of us set off down to the inlet, which required us to pass through a copse. As we approached, a branch suddenly fell from one of the trees and crashed to the ground. I'll admit it was a bit odd as there was, uncharacteristically, no wind that day, but it was not something that you would normally consider a concern. But the Kurd leading our little party stopped dead in his tracks and stared long and hard at the trees, unslinging his rifle from his shoulder as he did so. I couldn't for the life of me see what had alarmed him, the copse was perhaps a dozen trees and we could clearly see through them, so there seemed no need to worry about walking into an ambush. But the scout stood stock still and watched. Then he turned and indicated that we should take a different, much longer route to the river.

'Djinn,' he said, and led off.

I looked with incredulity at one of the other Kurds, who gave a shrug and a sheepish grin. A djinn is a spirit from folklore. To have a heavily armed squad add ten minutes – including a scramble up a sheer rock face – to their march, in burning sunshine and intense heat, because an evil spirit had just warned us off seemed bizarre. But that's what we did. It did mean we enjoyed the swim all the more when we got to the bathing point, though we had to be careful not to go out too far as Daesh would be able to see us, and they had a habit of shooting dushkas at swimmers.

The only time anything at all happened in the real world (as opposed to the spirit one) was on the night of 9 August. Daesh tried to send a patrol across and up our inlet, but the flanking positions on the hilltops spotted them through their thermal scopes and gave them a warm reception with their machine guns. We were slightly put out. If they'd held their fire until the enemy had been in our range they would have been caught on the shore between the fire from three positions and cut to bits. As it was, they scooted back out into the river and that was that.

Del Gesh and I spent our days helping out with chores, on guard and practising our Kurdish. I also began dreaming up ideas of what we should be doing, something that I would do throughout my time in Rojava. In this case, it was using boats to at least keep an eye on what Daesh was up to over the river, or, even better, sending raiding parties across to lay mines and harass the streams of traffic that ran day and night. The Kurds listened politely, agreed it was an interesting idea and then waited for me to drop it. To be fair, they had enough on their plate.

The situation to our north in Turkey had become extremely serious. Daesh had already launched attacks against Rojava from there, and in late July fighting had resumed between the PKK and the Turkish Army after a two-year ceasefire when peace talks broke down. The government of President Erdoğan, deeply nationalistic and with a strong Islamic bent, launched a major offensive against a number of Kurdish majority towns and cities in the south and east of the country. This had, in turn, caused Kurdish communities to rise in rebellion and form militias to try to protect themselves. We now faced the prospect of an attack if the Turks decided to intervene in Syria.

After a month or so guarding the inlet it was becoming apparent that nothing much was going to happen. Del Gesh and I figured we had done enough to establish ourselves as reliable in the eyes of the Kurds and thought it might be time to move on. I knew I had the job in the media department in prospect, and decided it was time to start making noises about taking up that role. Our tabor commander sent a message up the chain of command, and within a couple of days we received orders to report back to Karatchok for reassignment. We said goodbye to the guys in the squad, who were a great bunch and had done a good job of teaching us about their culture and language, and headed for the Karatchok military camp, located on a mountain just up the road from the academy.

Where we waited.

Just as the military guys found that their advice was not wanted, I found that the media department had their own way of doing things and did not seem interested in anyone else joining their outfit. Renas, my original contact, was on assignment and had asked for me to stick around until he got back, so I waited. Karatchok has a reputation for that, as it is the primary transit depot for troops waiting to deploy to new units. Even the Kurds call it *the waiting place.* I was fortunate that there were a number of interesting characters also stuck there, as they were the only distraction available while we spent our time sitting staring at the view down onto the plains and gradually going insane. A number of the foreigners were waiting to leave the country; some of them had been at Karatchok for well over a month and were, as a consequence, thoroughly disgruntled. One in particular, an Australian named Amed, got so aggravated that he threw his pack on his back and set off to hitch-hike back to his sabotage unit, which led to a proper Keystone Cops chase as the Kurds set off in vehicles to bring him back. They were thwarted when Amed turned off the road and headed across the fields. They eventually caught up with him seven miles later and convinced him to come back, on the promise that they would be shifting him out to Iraq in a few days.

After two weeks, I had had enough. Del Gesh was going to a sabotage tabor and I was fed up with waiting to be used sensibly. Another foreigner, a New Zealand veteran named Welat, was heading out to rejoin a sniper tabor he had been with and I asked him if I could tag along. I had never fired a scoped rifle in my life, but I thought there would be other roles that I could play in the tabor. The snipers of the Mobile Brigade are guaranteed to be where the action is during major campaigns, and so I figured that if I liked the unit it wouldn't be a bad place to try to take an active part in the conflict.

It took us several days to reach the unit as we were bounced around several bases in Rojava. I had the opportunity to talk with an Iranian Kurd who spoke very good English, and he was very keen to spell out his confusion as to why the West seemed to be so indifferent to the Syrian Kurds' struggle:

'Please, you must tell the people in the West about us. For the first time in generations the Kurdish people have hope. And we are scared. In the past, when things looked good for us things became terrible – we think this is going to happen again!

'We need the West to recognise our situation and help us. The airstrikes are very good but now we must think of what comes next. We have many things in common in our society and culture with America and Europe, we could be such good friends. And I think you need good friends here.

'We know that there are problems with politics and that Turkey is the West's ally against Russia, but Turkey helps Daesh, and Daesh wants to see all of us dead!

'We talk about Kurdistan, but this land has many people – Kurds, Arabs, Turkmen, Assyrians – and we must all live together. We must make a new country.

'Please tell the people in America and Europe about us. Without help many people will die and things will be worse than ever for the people here and in the West.'

This conversation got me thinking about the political and social problems in the region. There can be no denying that the issue of a future Kurdistan is immensely complicated. Many Kurds talk of the four regions being united, but with these regions spread across Syria, Iraq, Iran and Turkey it is an impossible dream, especially given the political divides among the Kurds. But if the West fails to help address the issues surrounding the Kurdish question, the future will be even more uncertain. And bloody.

In my view, a key factor that the West needed to deal with was the aggressive ideology of the political movement in Rojava. At that time, the only foreign representatives were from international communist organisations – the die-hards who thought that history could be proven wrong, that true communism had never been properly tried. As a result, their support was directed towards those in Rojava who followed their ideological leanings, in effect the Apogee old guard who had joined in the early days, in the 1980s, before Western anarchist and libertarian ideas began to gain currency. These elements would loudly declaim that Stalin hadn't been a bad guy at all. I can't pretend to be much of a political theorist, but it seems to me that to combine Stalinist communism, with its emphasis on strict centralisation, with anarchism's decentralist ideas would only lead to confusion and widely differing interpretations by different power blocs within the movement.

There were more moderate elements, who recognised the need for a progressive social democratic system and compromise in the party's old attitudes. If Western organisations and governments could identify the moderate members within the parliamentary system and direct assistance efforts through those channels, it might have been possible both to assist military efforts against ISIS and encourage greater liberalism within the broader movement and in the region.

Welat and I eventually washed up at a specialist unit, an armoured assault tabor, for a couple of days before we transferred to the snipers. This unit was famous among the foreign volunteers as it was unique in a number of ways. Firstly, it contained a large number of foreigners. Most tabors had become wary of having more than a couple of foreigners as it tended to create division and damage cultural integration, which negatively influenced combat performance – a polite way of saying that most Kurdish commanders considered foreigners a royal pain in the arse. A commander who lost a foreigner under his command would also, certainly at that time in the war, be subject to the equivalent of court martial, loss of command and even prison.

But the commander of this unit was positively anxious to recruit foreigners and enthusiastic about allowing them to go into combat. His standard roar of 'Heval [fill in name], are you ready to FIGHT?' was heard by most of us at some time or another, and he admitted that several years in the West had given him an appreciation for Western culture and music. As the unit was largely composed of Sorani-speaking Kurds from Iraq, it was viewed as something of an anomaly by the rest of the YPG, who spoke Kurmanji Kurdish or Arabic (and later Assyrian or Turkish, as people from those ethnicities joined). Recruiting new members from their own ethnic group to keep the unit up to strength was a problem for them. This need was met nicely by foreign volunteers.

Another important draw of the unit was that it was one of the only armoured vehicle tabors in the YPG. In September 2015, armoured vehicles were few and far between and this tabor held most of the available stocks of armoured Hummers, which were used as personnel carriers in assaults on Daesh positions and as ambulances for evacuating casualties from the battlefront. In short, they were guaranteed to be in the thick of it, which was where most foreigners wanted to be.

This unit gives a great example of the situation that the Kurds were in at this time. The tabor was one of the critical battle units and had a total of six armoured Hummers. Of these, four were operational, meaning that the vehicles would start, but were unlikely to be able to run very far, if at all. The vehicles had all been captured from Daesh, who in turn had captured them from the Iraqi Army, and, as can be imagined, they had seen a lot of very hard use. In fact, any conventional military force would have sent these heaps for scrap long ago. I sent a picture I took of them to a friend of mine in the US

Army. He replied that the guys in his barracks had laughed long and hard at the state of the things. They had been shot to bits, the windows were fractured and splintered, and I heard of at least one case where a driver had been killed by a shot through the windscreen as the bulletproof glass had been replaced with a standard windscreen. But at that time they were the best the YPG had.

5

'Snipers'

September/October 2015

We finally arrived at our destination, the sniper tabor of the Mobile Brigade. I was pleased at the choice I had made. Though the other units I had passed through were generally very good, a number were not, and I had heard tales from other foreigners about how some units suffered from a lack of discipline, and even how some tabors viewed foreign volunteers as little more than an opportunity to steal interesting toys and gadgets. The snipers were a long way away from that.

At the time I joined it was a small and tight group, only eighteen strong and all Kurdish, with an additional half-dozen women fighters. The snipers were renowned for their discipline and were considered an elite unit within the YPG. In fact, any higher commander in the organisation had almost certainly served time in a sniper tabor at some point in their career; it was considered an important development ground for future leaders. Snipers were expected to maintain the highest standards and, according to the democratic confederalist creed, any failure to do so could see a soldier sent to another unit with an indelible black mark against their name. Most ordinary soldiers aspired to a place in the snipers – in the coming days this would manifest itself on occasion as resentment when troopers found out I was one of the venerated few, but this turned into respect as I became better known.

It was a mixed blessing that two of the group spoke excellent English. I say mixed, because while it was a real benefit for getting a better understanding of the YPG, their ideology and their military experience, as it would be later when I would see combat alongside them, my Kurdish, marginal at best, atrophied. This was purely down to me as I could have pushed my own learning, but did not.

We were fortunate in our barracks. Most units in the Mobile Brigade tended to have no fixed home and as such moved between a range of houses across large areas of Rojava, never being allowed to settle. When I arrived, the tabor was in the process of having a house custom-built as its base. This meant we had just one bare concrete room to live in while the builders worked. We also had to squeeze our entire arsenal into this room as there was nowhere else secure to store anything – and having civilians walking around with possible access to weapons and explosives is not a good idea in anyone's book, especially when they might well be sympathetic to one of the other factions.

The women snipers were housed in a separate compound along with their colleagues from other tabors. Although some units were single sex, most were mixed. To avoid complications while in barracks, the YPJ lived in their own area and met up with their male colleagues to train and conduct processes such as tac mil. While visits to your comrades of the other gender were perfectly acceptable and expected out of politeness, it was not the done thing to visit the barracks of the opposite sex alone.

This all changed when conducting combat operations. Though generally men and women sleeping in close proximity was prohibited, it was understood that living in the field was an exceptional circumstance and that the rules required some flexibility. As snipers normally worked in pairs it wasn't unusual for a man and a woman to work together as a team, though assignment to a partner was never a fixed affair and you would usually work with different snipers on each mission.

Generally young – most of the YPJ snipers in the unit were under twenty – it was easy to misjudge these girls. With their penchant for pink Hello Kitty socks and colourful keffiyeh head wraps, they could sometimes look and act like the giggling teenagers that they were. But that disguised the fact that these girls were accomplished snipers, some with dozens of kills and several years of combat experience. You would underestimate them at your peril, and I would soon learn to respect their knowledge of their weapons and how to use them.

In terms of how we operated, though the YPG used the term sniper, we were more in the role known as designated marksmen in Western militaries. In other words, we would be deployed in pairs to support an infantry unit with long-range covering and suppressive fire. Kurdish snipers tended to operate far forward in comparison with snipers in a conventional army, often right alongside the soldiers they were supporting. As a result, they tended to suffer heavy casualties and many of their most famous members had fallen in the epic struggle for Kobane and other defensive battles.

Our weapon of choice was the Dragunov rifle. Every single one of us was issued with this famous design, which was subject to a level of reverence among the troopers, who thought of it as a sort of wonder-weapon capable of remarkable levels of accuracy. In reality, it is dated and limited, with some unpleasant shooting qualities, and is far surpassed by other more modern weapons. However, it is reliable, much tougher than its more accurate counterparts and – here is the real genius of the original Soviet designer – capable of use by troops with low levels of training. In the right hands it is a highly effective weapon and a number of the Kurdish snipers, as well as Daesh, were very skilled in its use, inflicting a considerable death toll on their enemies.

I had never so much as fired a full-power rifle (the Kalashnikov and M16 do not count as such), or a proper scoped weapon. In fact, when deciding on going to the snipers I had anticipated that I could fulfil some other role in the unit – machine-gunner, perhaps. There was a machine gun sitting gathering dust in the armoury, and I spent two days getting it back into pristine condition. However, the tabor commander decided that he wasn't going to have any machine-gunners in the unit; we were snipers, so I was given my first Dragunov.

The key thing about this weapon is the scope. While the PSO-1 is a device with limitations, such as only a four-times magnification, it is extremely easy to use. A sniper has to learn the art of how to judge distance and assess windage (the effect of any breeze on the drift of the projectile) and then adjust their scope settings accordingly. He or she must understand how any particular scope is set to reflect these changes and how the scope interacts with a particular rifle and the projectile's trajectory. The longer the range, the more precise these adjustments have to be. The PSO gets round these challenges by being designed solely for use with the Dragunov and its 7.62mm bullet. Ideally this would be the special sniper bullet designed for the weapon, but lacking those (as we were), standard machine gun ammunition can be used, albeit with a certain loss of accuracy.

To judge distance, a small range-finder is marked beside the reticule. This means that range can be estimated by lining up a target or other object in a fraction of a second rather than relying on the shooter's experience. To adjust for the target, instead of having to work out the number of *clicks* necessary to line the scope up to the required distance, as is the case with most scopes, with the PSO-1 the shooter simply has to adjust the range-setter to a distance marked clearly on the drum – if the target is five hundred metres away, just set it to 5. It isn't a hugely accurate weapon in comparison to modern sniper rifles, but if your rifle and shooting are good, and you judge the conditions correctly, the Dragunov is easily effective to eight hundred metres, and even further with practice.

Welat showed me another trick to improve the weapon, which I subsequently performed on every one of these guns that I was issued during my time with the snipers. The trigger on the Dragunov is extremely rough for a precision weapon, generally needing a long pull to take up the slack and then a stiff amount of pressure to fire the rifle. However, removing the entire trigger mechanism is a comparatively simple matter. You can then file down the trigger catch to be much more sensitive. Theoretically, you could file it down to a hair trigger, but I wouldn't recommend that if you are going to be bouncing around in the back of a pick-up, as the fighters in the region travel.

For longer-range engagements, more in line with a proper sniper role, the YPG relied at that time on two weapons they had built themselves: the Zagros 12.7mm (.5 inch) and Şer 14.5mm heavy rifles. The Şer rifles had made their reputation in the defensive battles against Daesh, but now were largely kept in the armoury as the two-man weapon, more akin to a Second World War anti-tank gun, was simply not manoeuvrable enough for the mobile fighting that the YPG had been engaged in since the victory at Kobane. The Zagros, however, I used and loved. Again, with no experience of heavy-calibre rifles I had no benchmark to measure it against and I have been told by more experienced marksmen that in comparison to a modern Western design like the Barrett it is a real brute. But in this case my ignorance was bliss. I was big enough physically to handle the huge weapon with ease and, if properly braced and set, could consistently put a round through a metre-square window at seven hundred metres with no difficulty, other than the effect on my hearing. The weapon was made in local workshops alongside dushkas, and consisted of a heavy machine gun barrel fitted into a milled-steel block as a receiver. It may not have been as elegant as Western designs, but there was no denying its effectiveness, nor its popularity among the snipers who had perfected its use.

There was also another set of weapons that could be called on for long-range fire. Two Sako TRG22 rifles were in the tabor arsenal, with dedicated precision scopes and ammunition. The contrast with the Dragunov was marked, and also highlighted the issues of using such rifles. The TRG22 was a model designed for police snipers, and was capable of astonishing accuracy. The problem was that to utilise them properly required extensive training on both how to read environmental conditions throughout the bullet's trajectory and how to set the scope correctly for the individual shooter. Such skills require huge amounts of practice, and very few of the Kurds had the required experience. As a result these rifles saw little use except among the most seasoned of the snipers, and then only occasionally as they preferred to use the more familiar Dragunov or, if shooting to extreme range, the Zagros. The Sakos thus spent most of the time in their custom-fitted protective cases, and would be largely used by Western veterans who passed through the unit periodically and had the requisite skills.

The snipers also had a higher than average quantity of M16 rifles in the unit. Given the limitations of the Dragunov in close-quarters combat, we all carried a secondary weapon. Due to the fact that the M16 is a more accurate weapon than the Kalashnikov, snipers often were able to lay their hands on them as their secondary rifle. Many of these were fitted with Chinese knock-off ACOG scopes which, if they were of reasonable quality (some were dreadful), did make the weapon a very usable marksman's rifle that was better than the Dragunov at ranges up to five hundred metres, because of the negligible recoil. Beyond that distance the lighter

5.56mm bullet of the M16 carried less well than the 7.62mm of the Dragunov.

The M16s were rare and many of them had, like the Humvees, originally been given to the Iraqi army by the United States, before being captured in turn by Daesh and the Kurds. I would learn how many of the YPG viewed their personal weapons as a status symbol, though this ran contrary to their ideology and was treated with some disdain by most of the snipers. An example of the need for prestige could be seen in the issuing of weapons to the favourites of senior commanders, or young fighters with good connections within the party. If M16s were rare, then weapons like the M4 carbine were unicorn droppings. These would have been of real use to specialist combat units like the sabotage or sniper tabors, but would inevitably be in the hands of personal drivers, or the sort of hangers-on you would only see lounging around at command posts in the rear during combat operations. This is, I admit, far from an unusual situation and really is a part of human nature that the Apogee philosophy opposes. However, when you find yourself one minute being lectured about the evils of personal possession and having the same person crowing about how wonderful their new toy is the next, it is a tad irritating, especially when said person is almost certainly never going to use their weapon.

The M16s were often used with the addition of thermal night scopes; these show the heat of an object, and areas such as a human body literally glow within the reticule. As a result, this combination played a key role in the various tasks of the sniper tabors. In combat operations, snipers would go out to hunt Daesh, normally closing to less than one hundred metres before killing their target if possible; they would guide attacking infantry units, watching for possible ambushes; and mounted night guard in key positions that were liable to be attacked – the latter role would often mean pulling a four- to eight-hour watch.

We trained on the M16s and thermal scopes by hanging a lighted cigarette about seventy metres away and trying to shoot the glowing end off. I managed to knock three off clean with three shots, but the M16 is an easy weapon to use and the hot tips showed up as bright white dots in the scopes, making for easy targets.

Having been issued with my new rifle, I hoped that we would be able to practise regularly and that I would have the opportunity to get an idea of how it and the snipers operated. I was to be disappointed. The YPG, having sprung up from a people's defence militia, and sourcing most of its weapons and ammunition from captured stocks, was loath to expend their precious reserves in military training exercises. This conformed to the Apogees' belief that the moral outweighs the physical. For them, structured commitment surpassed other battlefield considerations and, as such, their training consisted almost entirely of classroom lessons on their own political theory and the writings of Öcalan. In other words, political indoctrination.

Now, I am a firm advocate of the necessity of giving troops a sense of *esprit de corps*; without a determination to fight and a steadfast belief in the cause, equipment means nothing. The collapse of the Iraqi army, even with its modern American tanks and weapons, in the face of ISIS, demonstrated this basic principle of war only too clearly. To face down such a determined enemy means you have to have comparable, even superior morale. But to think that political lectures can take the place of actual combat exercises and practice is ridiculous.

My attitude towards this situation differed depending on whom I was discussing it with. With the Kurds, I would accept the need to understand their political theories, but would still express strong reservations that such an approach would be effective. Aggressive criticism would not get the point across. Later in my time in Syria I would encounter young foreign ideologues – normally with no real combat experience – who espoused the same idea. I would not bother to conceal my scorn.

Our actual weapons training consisted of the odd morning heading out to an abandoned village where we would set up, fire perhaps five rounds at targets ranging between fifty and seven hundred metres and then head back to the barracks. If we were training on the M16 or Zagros, it would be zeroed by the instructor and then we would be expected to hit the targets with that rifle. As a result, everyone would generally miss, or at least have a poor score. Welat, as a former soldier and security contractor, despaired of this and argued that we needed to use our own weapons or else zero the rifle in use each time and for each shooter for the lesson to actually be relevant. His complaints were dismissed and I could see that the YPG soldiers, though no doubt experienced in combat, had some major flaws in their tactical comprehension that could not be corrected because they would generally dismiss any instruction by foreigners as incorrect.

A great example (among several, I am afraid) concerned the purpose of the forward assist on the M16 rifle. This is a hangover from the Vietnam War, where the early models had problems with fouling, causing the weapon not to feed its ammunition properly. To solve this the manufacturer added a button on the right side of the gun that would when pushed physically force a trapped bullet into the breech, allowing it to fire. It's a simple and obvious device that, if you keep the weapon clean, isn't really necessary any more.

The YPG, however, refused to accept this. At some point they had been told that the forward assist was, in fact, a *sniper button*. If you wanted a bullet to have more velocity and accuracy you pushed the button while firing. In my time there I explained continually that this wasn't the case. Countless other foreign volunteers, many former soldiers with an intimate knowledge of the gun, would do the same. On several occasions I broke the weapon down, showing exactly how the forward assist worked. Nothing doing. The YPG's training taught them it was a sniper button, and nothing would convince them otherwise. I suspect that at some early point in the organisation's history an M16 had fallen into their hands. Some self-proclaimed expert had taken it upon himself to explain the weapon and, when asked what the bolt assist did, had made up the sniper button story.

It may seem that I am being overly critical, but this episode demonstrates a clear failing of the YPG and the Syrian Democratic Forces (SDF) more widely. In essence, their ideology and the perceived decadence and softness of the outside world led to a dangerous level of self-confidence that was, quite frankly, unjustifiable. They could not be corrected on their failings by outsiders and refused to assess objectively the lessons from the campaigns they had fought in defence of their territory. Instead, a mythology of their superiority as fighters was being crafted by the well-oiled propaganda machine: you would often hear the YPG boast that the tactics they had developed in Kobane were the best in the world, and that professional soldiers watched in envy as their combat prowess was demonstrated. This was delusion of the highest order. The consequences of drilling such nonsense into their soldiers' heads would later prove to be a major issue. But that was in the future.

In the meantime, we sat in our barracks and watched the border. The location of our tabor, and our apparent lack of activity, served another purpose, which I gradually became aware of as the summer faded into autumn. The Turkish border was perhaps two miles away and their tanks and positions were facing us. Quite often you could look through binoculars and find yourself staring straight down the barrel of a Turkish tank. A few miles further on, hedged by Turkish army bases, was a large refugee camp. When I first arrived my team leader, a highly experienced sniper, pointed it out and warned me to look out for any developments at the camp.

'When we took Sari Kani from Al Nusra,' he told me, 'they ran to Turkey and were given that camp. The Turks will use them against us if they get the chance.'

I can't say if there was any truth in this, but I certainly kept a close watch on the camp whenever I pulled guard duty.

Between our training and guard duty, there was not a great deal to do. We spent the time either talking with our Kurdish colleagues or just sitting and watching the world go by. Sometimes we were treated to the sight of the tanks and armoured vehicles of the neighbouring heavy weapons tabor, which would come out and heave themselves around the field behind our house. It was a collection of battered antiques, though lovingly maintained by the YPG as best they could, which demonstrated just how much of a shoestring the YPG was running on. The real oddities were the panzers, misshapen monsters with no two the same. The tanks and MTLB armoured personnel carriers were at least built for purpose and could shift themselves across rough terrain at speed. But watching the panzers crawling around made me feel sorry for the crews who had to man such lumbering hulks. Fortunately, they rarely had to be deployed to the front line as enough proper armoured vehicles had been captured from Daesh, or else from old Syrian army stocks.

One day as Welat and I watched one lumbering up and down in the field he turned to me and said:

'What I wouldn't give for twenty M113s. We could really kick arse with them.'

He had a very valid point. Twenty vehicles, less than a drop in the ocean of the military support being lavished on the Iraqi army or the KDP Peshmerga, would have revolutionised our offensive ability. I'm glad to say that modern armoured vehicles did start to reach the SDF eventually, but not until after my time in Syria had ended.

During this time some recently captured equipment was sent to us. Most noticeable, and which got the most attention, was a huge sniper rifle. This was a Chinese-made M99, chambered in 12.7 x 108mm, the same as our Zagros. But it was a semi-automatic, magazine-fed weapon, which allowed for much more rapid shooting. It also had a very expensive German scope, which was immeasurably superior to the cheap Chinese sights that we used with our heavy rifles. Needless to say, it caused a great deal of excitement among the snipers, who would all vie for the right to use it. I must admit I was not interested in the gun. Welat and I were more taken with another piece of equipment that had been brought in.

It was a top-of-the-range Canadian-made thermal scope. Our own thermals were adequate for the tasks we used them for, but this was on a whole other level. As we were able to use the internet on our phones Welat and I soon managed to identify the make and model, and discovered that it retailed for sixteen thousand dollars. And, apparently, this scope was one of several that the Kurds had managed to capture in the summer's fighting.

We got quite excited about the prospect of using the scope in conjunction with our Sakos, which could mean using those rifles at night to their maximum effective range of over a kilometre. The combination had immense potential. But once we told our comrades the value of the scope, who then passed it up the line, it was suddenly whisked away – probably to one of the rear-echelon types to preen over and show off.

One of the key topics that our Kurdish comrades wanted to discuss, apart from politics, was the attitude of the outside world both to them and their struggle. At that time, the US was still very lukewarm in their support for the YPG because of the importance of their relationship with Turkey. The Kurds were adamant that Turkey, and particularly the Erdoğan government, were actively supporting ISIS against them. As they put it:

'Daesh want to kill us and destroy the West. Turkey helps Daesh. They supply them with weapons and help their fighters come and go. How can they be friends of the West if they are helping the West's sworn enemies?'

I must admit, I didn't have an answer.

We were joined at the unit by a couple of British volunteers and now our training, which as I've said was fairly limited anyway, hit a road block when one day we piled off the back of our pick-ups, only to find that the house on whose roof we used to practise had acquired new residents.

Our team leader approached a woman who had come out to greet us.

'Hello,' he said. 'We practise here.'

'Hello,' she said. 'We live here.'

The reappearance of the former inhabitants meant that we had to find somewhere else to conduct weapon drills, which became more and more difficult as people returned to their homes and began to rebuild. The fall-off in training meant that our boredom had started to reach crisis levels, and soon the rest of the foreign volunteers departed for other units, and the promise of more action. But in truth it was nice to see that people were starting to return to the deserted villages now that they were sure the fighting was over. The debris and wreckage was rapidly cleared and within months communities were thriving again. Passing through one such hamlet, perched on the back of a pick-up, one of my Kurdish colleagues waved to the kids who always poured out to greet the SDF soldiers. He smiled.

'You know, just six months ago I was in this village, fighting. Daesh and us spent a month hammering each other,' he said.

He waved to more of the children as we drove past. Their mothers were doing their washing and other household tasks.

'It makes me happier than I can say to see these villages and towns come back to life like this. This is why we sacrifice ourselves. This is why we fight.'

But for months now there had been no fighting, except skirmishes out on the front line. The world was still trying to figure out what was to be done about Daesh and for them, more importantly, who was going to do it.

Of particular concern was the announcement in September that the Russians were going to deploy troops in Syria to assist their ally President Assad. Although there was an uneasy peace between the regime and the Kurds, no one was under any illusion that there wouldn't be a reckoning at some point in the future. Assad's dictatorship essentially summed up everything that was wrong with Syrian politics for the YPG, while for Assad it seemed unlikely that he could allow any form of power-sharing if he hoped to hang on to both his authority and his life.

The YPG, with their old Stalinist hang-up, had thought that the Russians would support them. The news that they had in fact committed unequivocally to Assad caused great consternation and, as the only person with any extensive experience of the outside world, I ended up being cross-questioned by the whole tabor about the implications.

'Will the Russians fight against us for Assad?'

'Well, Assad is Russia's man here. They are making it plain that they are backing him to retain power. So, if the Syrians come after us, Russia might help Assad, especially with air-strikes, weapons and supplies.'

Understandably, much brooding resulted.

'If they do support the Syrian army against us, will the West help us?'

'No. I'm sure that no one in the West will back us against the Russians at this time.'

This was before the Americans declared that the YPG were the best troops in theatre to fight ISIS, and the SDF umbrella group was still in the process of creation. In fact, the Americans seemed at that time to have more faith in the Free Syrian Army (FSA) forces fighting in Idlib and Aleppo. These had first consisted of the original Syrian army rebels who had started the war by rising up against the Assad regime. But by this point they had become thoroughly associated with Islamists who opposed ISIS, yet pretty much represented the same thing. Watching television one day I saw a news report about jihadists fighting Assad's forces around Damascus. The jihadists had the usual black flag flying over their troops and this confused me. I didn't know ISIS had reached the outskirts of the capital. Confused, I turned to one of the Kurds with me and asked:

'Daesh?'

'No,' he said, and then thought for a second.

'Like Daesh.'

It was then I began to refer to the FSA as *Daesh Light* and *I Can't Believe They're Not Daesh*. It might seem flippant, but to an outsider like me, the difference between the groups was negligible.

Though greater support from outside powers would start to become noticeable in the coming months, at that time the soldiers on the ground felt very lonely. For them, it seemed that they were fighting this war alone.

The fact remained that, despite the defeat of Daesh and Al Nusra in the region, our enemies were still able to reach in among us and wreak havoc. Two car bombs detonated in Sari Kani in September, and then we received orders that we were to send a team out to the foot of the Abdul Aziz mountain range. Daesh sympathisers within the civilian population had laid a landmine that had destroyed a YPG vehicle and killed a tabor commander. We were being sent to hunt them down.

On 29 October my team was deployed on the windswept plain to the north of the foothills. Though northern Syria is almost uniformly flat, the Abdul Aziz rears up and runs broadly east to west across central Rojava. Daesh had managed to push this far, and had then been driven back over the mountains. Unfortunately, the villagers in the area, of whom there were precious few, still thought that Daesh would be back and supported them.

Our orders were simple. We would be driven out at night and the lone village close to the ambush point was to be watched through thermal scopes. Anyone leaving the village and approaching the road would be closely observed from our hidden position. If they showed any sign of being armed or of planting mines we were to try to capture them or, if that wasn't possible, shoot them.

We watched over the course of two nights, but no one showed. Then we were suddenly recalled. We didn't know it, but a major operation was about to be launched.

6

Going to War – The Al Hawl Operation

November/December 2015

On 31 October 2015, my war started in earnest. We returned to our tabor and were ordered to head out to a command base where a horde of units had gathered for a briefing on an offensive. Our target: Al Hawl.

The attack on Al Hawl marked a new stage in the war. The YPG was now part of a broader organisation, the Syrian Democratic Forces, which comprised a number of additional militias from other ethnicities that had allied themselves with the Kurds to form the new coalition. Some were local tribal organisations, some were the military wings of political parties and some were local defence units that had sprung up in response both to Daesh and to the Assad regime. The Kurdish YPG would form the principal element of the organisation in my time there, but by the time I left in July 2016 Arab,

Assyrian and Turkmen units were participating more and more.

It was also the first time the YPG had been involved in a major offensive into territory that they had no wish to claim, it was a liberation of Arab areas outside of Rojava and a mark that we were now to carry the war against Daesh to the so-called caliphate rather than just recovering our own territory and defending it. This made for a joyous mood among the troops.

Having received our briefing from the commander, we saddled up and headed to an abandoned Syrian army base in Hasakah, where our forces were gathering for the attack. It was here that I was to see how the Kurds and Arabs did things slightly differently. We laagered up in a large parade square and immediately it was noticeable that the Kurdish and Arab units had separated themselves into two groups, each taking half of the campsite. The Arab tabors were composed exclusively of men, whereas the Kurdish YPJ women fighters were very obvious around the fires at our end of the campsite.

As is usual at such gatherings, the whole place rapidly descended into a party. The Kurdish men and women performed traditional dances, which involved forming a large circle, linking pinkie fingers, and going through a complicated series of memorised dance steps that matched the song blaring from every vehicle's sound system. At the other end of the campsite, the Arab fighters were playing their own music, at similar ear-destroying decibel levels, and just going nuts, from what I could see. These young men, recent recruits to the SDF, would prove to be brave fighters in spite of their lack of combat experience.

For the foreign volunteers, it was a joy. While the two groups were obviously not going to mix if they could avoid it, for us it was a smörgasbord of different experience as we all bounced from fire to fire in a happy Brownian motion, getting offers of food and tea everywhere we went.

It was while I was wandering around the camp that I ran into John Gallagher, the Canadian who I had first met at the safe house in Sulaymaniyah. He was part of 223, the tabor made up exclusively of foreigners that trained and fought as a Western military unit. We spent some time catching up and parted with the usual sentiments to keep an eye out for each other during the operation. I would not see him again: he was killed four days later, by a bullet to his pelvis. He died quickly from loss of blood, despite the best efforts of his team to save him.

The plan of attack was extensive. Two large battle groups, one from Hasakah and one from Shingal (also known as Sinjar), advanced from east and west to hit Al Hawl from both sides. My sniper squad was part of the drive from Hasakah, which would envelop a large quantity of territory before moving in on the target itself, clearing the villages caught in our trap. It was, in essence, a blitzkrieg launched by Toyota Hiluxes.

The operation was comparatively straightforward and we swept over most of the villages in our encirclement, encountering gradually stiffening resistance offered by a rearguard of suicide troops. Daesh's liberal use of vehicle-based improvised explosive devices (VBIEDs – or suicide car bombs), mortars, Katyusha rockets and anti-tank missiles, plus a worrying number of extremely well-constructed bunkers inside innocent-looking village houses, gave the impression that we were facing a well dug-in foe. In fact, the area was fairly lightly defended and the issues we did face were normally attributed by the Kurds to inadequate air support from the coalition rather than an acknowledgement of their own tactical failings, as well as to an underestimation of Daesh's level of competence, which could be highly professional.

For me, the operation meant a few firsts, including the first time I faced a suicide vehicle, got mortared, got rocketed and got shot at with a heavy machine gun. It was the start of what would be an increasingly dangerous progression, as the fighting in each succeeding campaign became more intense and brutal.

The 1st of November, Day One of the operation, would see me deployed supporting an Arab tabor. Another sniper and I were given a stretch of road that headed to a large town to watch. We set up our positions on the roof of a mud house, with the machine gun from the tabor on top of a neighbouring house. We overlooked an abandoned Daesh police checkpoint about four hundred metres away and we were simply there to provide part of the defensive line holding the circle as the main thrust from the Hasakah brigade moved to complete its part of the encirclement of a vast swathe of territory centred on Al Hawl. We weren't expecting anything serious to happen. That assessment proved to be wrong.

The day had settled down into a simple routine. The other sniper and I built rough defensive positions with mud bricks, which didn't provide a lot of cover – in fact, we were horribly exposed. But our view was good and we could see for kilometres. The machine-gun team rapidly lost interest in the proceedings and left their rooftop to sit on the ground around a fire and drink tea. As there was only one ladder between us, and they had it, I figured it would be wise to check for my quickest route out. The back of the house appeared to have some sort of runoff, leaving the ground a bit of a quagmire. It was a ten-foot drop, but I was happy that if I had to bug out quickly I could jump off the roof into the mud and head for the hills, with the house between me and the anticipated direction of attack.

Though it was late in the year, the weather was still warm and the Syrian sun is merciless. Lying on a roof in its full glare is tiring, and as the hours slowly ticked away my mind settled into a blank state as I scanned my designated arc. A yelled warning from my partner sniper roused me. To my right, coming from the town, was a rapidly approaching dust cloud that marked the passage of a high-speed vehicle. And that could only mean we were about to be hit by a suicide car bomb.

I lined my Dragunov up on the point in the road where the vehicle would become visible to me. The road there had been partially blocked by small berms of earth that forced any vehicle to slow down to negotiate them. Those Daesh defences would now slow down the attacker and force it to present its side to us. At that stage in the war the SDF had minimal anti-armour weapons, limited principally to the RPG. And those were far too inaccurate to hit a fast-moving vehicle at a range that would save the shooter from any large explosion caused by the payload. The snipers were the only ones who had a reasonable chance of stopping such an attack, by using precision fire to try to hit tyres or drivers. I planned to engage the vehicle at about eight hundred metres, where it would crest a small slope and come into my line of sight, and then continue firing until it passed the checkpoint. If the vehicle was still moving at that point we weren't going to be stopping it and I would be testing my escape route.

I settled in, slowed my breathing, set the range on my scope and tried to focus on the target area. Unfortunately, I was distracted by an almighty commotion sounding off just to my right. The machine gun team, after first wandering over to have a look at what we were shouting about, had gone into a panic. There followed something akin to a scene from an Ealing comedy. One guy tried to climb the ladder to get back on the roof to the machine gun, but in his haste knocked it over. He and another fighter both grabbed the ladder and started a tug of war trying to get it righted. Then, when that was finally sorted, the two of them tried to climb up at the same time and promptly fell off!

I can look back and laugh at this now, but it wasn't so funny at the time. Especially when the car bomb hove into view. It was a Hummer, with huge slabs of armour plate across the whole vehicle. A great beetle hump had been welded to the back and obviously contained a huge quantity of explosives: several tons, I would estimate. The only spots of vulnerability I could identify through my scope were the tyres, which had armoured boxes protecting them, and a tiny slit in the front that was the driver's view port. Knowing how thick Hummer tyres are, I doubted that even if I were to hit them my dinky 7.62mm bullet would cause enough damage to stop the vehicle before it destroyed one of our positions. But if I aimed for the driver's tiny aperture I could perhaps distract him. Getting a round through it was a million to one shot, but strikes close to his face might make the driver to flinch or else cause splinters of steel to fly off from the impact – not a pleasant experience to endure. So that's what I shot at.

The Hummer was travelling at considerable speed and though I and my fellow sniper placed round after round into it, which were quickly added to by the machine gun crew (who had finally got themselves sorted) and positions on the other side of the road, the speeding bomb ate up the distance. I became aware of someone screaming my name.

'Botan! Go! Run!' my fellow sniper was bellowing at me.

My reply would have been considered gross insubordination in a professional military organisation. Fortunately, the YPG isn't one.

bang 'No thank you.' *bang* 'I'm OK here.' *bang* 'Don't worry, I'll . . . ' *bang* ' . . . run away when it's time.' *bang*

And the moment was fast approaching. The Hummer slowed to manoeuvre around the roadblocks. I had, at best, enough seconds for two more rapid shots and then it was time to go, if running from a maniac in a car full of explosives across open fields was much of an option. Fortunately, it didn't come to that. With an almighty blast the Hummer's rear tyre blew out, causing the vehicle to lurch sideways and stall. Our team commander, two hundred metres further up the road, had placed a perfect shot with his Zagros rifle.

'See? I told you it was OK,' I shouted at my partner as I reloaded, and then proceeded to join the wall of fire that was rising to a crescendo as everyone with a weapon started shooting at the immobilised VBIED.

Smoke started to trickle from the stricken vehicle. The driver got the engine started and managed to get a few lurches out of it, and then . . .

FFFFWWWOOOOOOOOPPPP

It is difficult to explain a big explosion, especially when you are only four hundred metres away and staring straight at it. I could see everyone in my sightline instinctively curl down as the light and heat hit them. And that's what it was, for what seemed like a huge period: just light and heat. But I didn't look away. I wanted to see it.

The shockwave races towards you, kicking up the dust and a wave of debris. And, as it reaches you, the noise. Like a thunderclap right by your head. And a great ball of flame that swirls up into the sky. The blast physically picked me up six inches off the roof where I was lying prone and dropped me back down. With hindsight, I realise I was lucky to have been positioned on an old mud-brick building rather than a modern, breeze-block construction. The mud buildings are tremendously resilient to shock and projectiles, whereas concrete tends to shatter. If I had been on a breeze-block house it probably would have collapsed under me.

The bellow of the blast grumbled away and we all screamed in joy, a celebration of our survival and the enemy's demise. A man had died, but we had lived. He had come to kill us. We'd killed him.

Then it was time to duck, because it had started raining bloody great lumps of metal.

The patter of debris finally stopped and we emerged grinning from our foetal positions. And I was to find another delight awaiting. As the explosion rumbled away I suddenly heard an overstressed engine whirring behind me. I turned to see that a YPG Hummer had crashed off the road a few hundred metres away, almost turning onto its side. As I watched, the driver climbed out, presenting me with a joyous sight. It was my old friend Del Gesh. He'd been driving the Hummer towards our positions, on high alert because they had been warned about a suicide vehicle in the neighbourhood; hearing the storm of weapons fire had got him and his crew really jumping. He was then confronted with an explosion so big right in front of him that it looked like someone had just dropped a nuclear bomb. He had, understandably, swerved and crashed.

He was somewhat nonplussed by what had happened. He was even less happy as my gloating laughter and greeting floated across the fields to him.

'You WANKER.'*

The next day I was put into the neighbouring position with my team commander, who had made the shot. Close to where he had fired from, a huge lump of twisted armoured plate, a good 15mm thick, had crashed down after the explosion. Even when destroyed, the VBIEDs were potentially lethal as these great pieces of steel rained down over a wide area, and later campaigns I fought in would see them expand to a huge size with the corresponding risk of debris hitting you at their destruction. Still, the wrecked armour plate did not go to waste. We used it to make a position that overlooked the

* When we met up at a later date, he said to me: 'Of all the places I had to crash, you had to be there! You cunt.' And I always thought Canadians were polite.

town and it protected us from any return fire. There wasn't much of that, so we watched our dushkas putting fire into the town.

As I have already mentioned, dushkas come in a range of calibres, but their use is worthy of more detailed description. The gunners take great care to fire them a single round at a time, as these weapons were intended for accurate fire rather than hosing down the horizon. The gunner would carefully adjust his aim depending on the fall of shot until it was on target. The dushkas might have been based upon anti-aircraft guns, yet they were quite effective as a support weapon in the sort of war we were waging. They were certainly better than heavier weapons we had available, which suffered from the crews not being able to train properly because of a lack of ammunition.

The campaign went reasonably well for the first week or so, but Daesh were far from finished and we found that many of the little villages, often only a handful of houses, had a position with a couple of Daesh who intended to die defending them. Many of them were apparently Russian-speakers, judging by the large amounts of literature that we discovered. It was in one of these little nondescript places that John was killed. Mines and booby traps were also an ever-present threat, as was regular mortaring and rocketing. Two days running I had encounters with 120mm mortars that were uncomfortably close. While I was lounging against the corner of a building waiting to see if I was to be assigned to an attack, a bomb landed just next to me on the other side of the corner. The building (again, one of the tough mud builds) absorbed the blast and shrapnel, only leaving me with ringing ears. The next day I was on the corner of the same building, this time on the side that had been hit. Having admired the fragments imbedded in the wall, I was lounging with my rifle, again waiting for orders, when a bomb fell pretty much where I'd been standing the day before! I couldn't decide whether someone was out to get me, or watching my back.

When my orders eventually came, I learned that I and another sniper were to support a tabor that had got into trouble. The unit in question was a kilometre further up in a village they'd just taken; they had started taking heavy fire from an adjacent village, where Daesh evidently had a substantial force. To get there we would have to run down an open road with no cover, surrounded by cleared fields and the usual smattering of small farmhouses, any of which could hold the enemy. We would be the only thing moving across the open terrain, and sure to draw the eye, so were told: 'Go quick. Don't stop.'

The two of us and a guide set off. Though my fitness had been very good when I first arrived in Syria, several months of sedate living and the relaxed training regimen the Kurds enjoyed had had a detrimental effect on my running. This was not helped by the fact that I was carrying a Dragunov, a Kalashnikov, hundreds of rounds of ammunition for both, and grenades. My fellows were in as bad shape as me, and by six hundred metres we had gradually slowed from a sprint to a walk, all gasping for breath. Of course, this was when the heavy machine gun opened up on us.

A .50 calibre bullet is a hell of a thing, especially when it's tracer and winging by your head. It is also a great impetus to get yourself shifting. We all set off running bent over as the gunner, fortunately aiming high enough that his rounds went roaring overhead, was joined by what seemed like every Daesh within two kilometres opening up on us with everything they had. We pelted down the road, a huge volume of fire whizzing by or kicking up splinters at our feet as rounds ricocheted around us. I honestly cannot understand how none of us was hit, though I would later pick a number of rock splinters out of my legs and hands.

We tore into the village with fire chasing us the whole way. An earth berm had been thrown up across the road and we dived down behind it, gasping. The machine-gunner who had started the shooting evidently didn't want to let us go, and continued to pour fire into the mound. I lay flat on my back as the heavy rounds thudded into the dirt and threw clods down onto me. To stop dirt getting onto my scope I tucked my rifle across my chest and put my arm over the sight. We'd made it, and I was quite happy to wait for our antagonist to vent his fury against the berm before moving again, so I settled my head against the ground and waited. My companion sniper looked at me and said:

'Botan. Stay down.'

I had to laugh at that.

Eventually the gunner got bored and stopped shooting at us. I was happy he had wasted a considerable amount of ammunition trying to tag us and, after about a half hour of staying out of sight, we made a sprint to a rooftop position that housed the commander of the tabor. I set up with a view across open fields, Daesh being located in houses scattered across the district. Things quietened down except for the occasional sniper round that kept us all down low and in cover. Naturally, it was our job to return the favour. I slid across the roof, settled my rifle so that I could watch a house nine hundred metres away across the fields and set myself up to wait. This is much harder to do than you may think. The weather was cooling as the winter drew on and the temperature was a much more pleasant 30 degrees Celsius or so. But the sun was still fierce and lying on a concrete roof in these conditions makes for great sleeping conditions, especially when you are getting woken up every night for guard duty and quite often by random mortaring. Still, falling asleep would not be doing your job, so you battle through, force your eyes to stay open and watch. And occasionally, it pays off.

A flicker of movement caught my eye and I twitched my rifle round to examine it. A kilometre away a man with a rifle was running for the house I had been observing. I watched the movement of the long grass around his legs as he ran, to judge the wind speed and direction, and steadied my breathing to slow my heartbeat so that the vibration didn't interfere with the shot. The target had just about reached the garden of the house, which had a number of trees, and had slowed to a jog as he moved into their cover. I adjusted my aim and squeezed the trigger. A second later he fell flat on his face among the shadows. I can't say whether I hit him, or if he had dived down from the bullet passing him, as he was now obscured by the foliage. I continued to watch for a long time, in case I had the opportunity for a second shot. But I saw no more movement.

The next day I became involved in a bizarre, long-range gun battle. Many people think that a sniper's job is what they have seen in the movies: one shot, one kill. While that is without doubt the ideal, there are many more roles a sniper can play, such as observation and area denial. Certainly, knowing a sniper is in the area slows everyone down, makes them much more careful about exposing themselves and generally creates a tense situation. In short, just having people know a sniper is in the area is an impediment to normal actions. Watching a village that was occupied by Daesh through my binoculars, I could see an armed group engaged in a discussion in an alleyway between two houses. The range was thirteen hundred metres, which is the theoretical limit of what you can hit with the Dragunov. At that range, men look not much bigger than ants in the PSO scope and using standard machine gun rounds, as we did, further degraded the accuracy. In addition, I was standing behind a water tank, and to even see the target area I had to balance precariously on a breeze block. A stable firing position it certainly was not. But once our request for an airstrike was turned down (the coalition was being sparse with their favours at this early point in the Hawl campaign), and I had been denied permission to crawl out through the grass to get close enough to make an effective shot, I decided I might as well try to disrupt this mothers' meeting.

The range meant that my bullet would take nearly two seconds to reach them and the wind was creating dust devils in the village itself, so estimating the air current was beyond my limited expertise. But I must have been reasonably close, as all four figures flinched and ran for cover behind the buildings. I was pleased with the effect; it was the best I could hope for. But I managed to do better with my next shot. Watching the alleyway, I could just make out, even at that range, one of the

Daesh peeping out from around the corner. With hindsight, I should of course have waited, let them calm down and come back out in the open. Still, as the range would never let me get a decent shot in, I figured I would take another pot shot to keep them hopping. To my surprise, and his, the round hit the wall on the opposite side of the alley, throwing a cloud of dirt into his face. The round might have missed him by a metre and a half, but that's close enough to scare the life out of you.

My opponent didn't appreciate my attention, and suddenly jumped out into the alleyway and started shooting wildly with his AK. My first reaction on seeing his firing was to step off my breeze block and warn the squad I was with that we were taking fire. And then I laughed when I realised he had zero chance of hitting me. I took up my position again, sighted in on my crazed antagonist and squeezed off another shot. This time he saw my muzzle flash and stepped back around the corner. Then he came back and resumed trying to shoot me. Credit for effort, but not for thinking: if I couldn't hit him with a weapon much better suited for longer-range shooting, firing an AK was just wasting ammunition. I fired half a dozen rounds as I was now taking the opportunity to practise my long-range shooting rather than trying to hit any specific target, while he must have burned through several magazines in reply. This might seem a waste of effort, but as practice with the Dragunov had been extremely restricted I thought I might as well try to make up a tiny bit of ground. It also meant that the Kurdish commander could call up that we were engaged in a gunfight, which would get the coalition's attention. An hour later a bomb fell behind the houses where the Daesh guys had gone to ground – and that was that.

The low number of airstrikes early in this campaign caused some comment among the Kurds, who took it as an attempt by the Americans to destroy the YPG by forcing them to engage Daesh in slugging infantry battles. I was inclined to point out that the US Air Force was in trouble for recently destroying a Médecins Sans Frontières hospital in Afghanistan and were going to be very careful with airstrikes as a result, especially as the requests were being called in by local forces rather than Special Forces directors who were, at this stage, almost unknown in Syria. However, as resistance built up we started getting a lot more support. This was graphically – and, for me, hysterically – illustrated one day when a Kurdish fighter was angrily castigating me (as if I could do anything about it) that the Americans were not doing anything to help us. We were bogged down in front of a village that was putting out a hell of a lot of fire and were well and truly stuck. Just as his rant reached its crescendo, an American A10 attack jet swooped through the low cloud and obliterated the building holding up our advance.

'You were saying?' I had to ask.

This was my introduction to this wonderful aircraft and I would be both thankful for and awed by it on many occasions in my time in Syria. I've seen airstrikes from just about everything in the coalition's inventory, and the A-10 and the AC-130 are what you want when things are getting sticky. The A-10, also known as the Hog because of its blunt, ugly snout, is an attack plane that has been the supreme ground support aircraft since it was introduced in the 1970s. It carries a huge array of weaponry, with a massive 30mm rotary cannon as its pièce de résistance. The huffing roar of this gun is fantastic for putting the fear of God into an enemy, or for picking up the morale of troops who know the sound means that, somewhere out there, people who mean them harm are having hell delivered to them.

The AC-130 gunship is also a ground support aircraft, and a real beast of one at that. Based on the huge C-130 Hercules transport, these are then fitted with hundreds of millions of dollars' worth of thermal sights and 25mm rotary cannons, 40mm guns and even a 105mm howitzer. The gunship would circle the battlefield, able to see everything with its electronic sensors and then deliver immense firepower that was tailored to what the crew thought was necessary with its vast battery. Although it isn't much use in a high-tech battleground with air defences, against an enemy like Daesh such a weapon is the most flexible and devastating imaginable.

As a side note, at the time of writing the USAF is looking at how to replace the A-10. On behalf of every grunt who ever got support from one of these beautiful birds – don't. Build new ones if you have to, but don't pretend some high-tech space jet can do the job as well as the Hog. Because if it ain't broke, why spend a fortune to fix it?

The importance of the airstrikes to the turning of the war was crucial, not that many in the YPG would admit it. In fact, I can only recall one occasion when I heard a Kurd admit that without the overwhelming superiority provided by the coalition's air power, they would have been destroyed.

My team commander and I set out to support a tabor that was holding the front line. Our position was in a hedge line where we could overlook a nearby village and the road that led to it. It gave us good cover and an excellent observation point, but the range was fifteen hundred metres and therefore beyond my weapon's capabilities. Fortunately, my colleague was an expert with the Zagros, so on this day we would act more as a traditional sniper team, with him shooting and me spotting his fall of shot and watching for other threats and targets.

Moving up through the surrounding buildings to get to the location, I examined three Daesh who had been killed the previous night. Our tabor colleagues had closed to within a hundred metres and, equipped with M16s and thermal scopes, had killed the three men in less than a second – a textbook SDF night sniper mission. They were sprawled in the barn where they'd been killed, and though it is difficult to generalise they did not look like Arabs. Two were blond with blue eyes, and I assumed they were from Russia or the Caucasus. The other had a much darker complexion; I would hazard a guess that he was from the subcontinent. The three of them had heeded the call for jihad and ended up here, gunned down in the dark by a Kurd. I'd be sympathetic, but for my deep hatred of what they'd chosen to stand for. Certainly the Kurds and Arabs of the SDF had little regard for our enemy – they routinely referred to Daesh as *çeta*, which translates as bandit or brigand, a reviled outcast.

We settled in and soon had the opportunity to engage the enemy. The village we were watching had a number of Daesh in it, and they had to scuttle across the open spaces as fast as they could, as we made the exposed areas lethal for them. Airstrikes had again been disallowed as the Americans believed there were civilians in the village. We didn't want to hit any buildings for the same reason, and this constrained the shots we could make. We kept harassing fire up all day, shooting at fleeting targets as they darted from cover to cover, and I got to see the lengths Daesh were going to in an attempt to try to thwart observation by coalition aircraft. A tanker truck pulled up a few kilometres away from the village we were targeting and I watched through my binoculars as the driver climbed out, opened the stopcocks and let fuel spill out onto the road. He set a small grass fire nearby, then was picked up by a motorbike and left. The truck was soon part of a huge conflagration that spiralled a dense column of filthy smoke into the air. All along the horizon similar clouds were forming as Daesh started fires across the battle zone to try to thwart our air support.

We continued to shoot at any armed man we saw, but the presence of a sniper is always a good incentive to stay hidden and the day drew on with less and less to see. With nothing to eat all day, my stomach was rumbling when suddenly the delicious smell of roasting meat blew across to me from the tabor. My mouth began to water and I turned to my colleague and asked if the infantry guys would remember us and bring over some of the meat, a rare treat. He lifted his eye from his scope, sniffed the air and made a grimace of disgust.

'They're burning the çeta,' he said. 'I told them to bury them.'

That's one hunger-suppression technique you don't hear advocated by the diet industry, but it is highly effective.

As the light began to fail we packed up our gear and headed back to our billet for the night. It was a five-mile hike, but the terrain was flat and the temperature in the dusk was pleasant so we walked without any problems despite the heavy load of weapons and ammunition. We walked in silence, until my colleague made an admission I never heard from any other Kurd.

'A year ago,' he said, 'we were fighting for survival. And we were finished. Daesh came at us like an army, with tanks and artillery and many, many men. They came in waves. And we fought them, but we were done. It was just time.'

He turned and looked at me.

'And then the airstrikes came. They came and crushed the tanks and the guns, killed Daesh in the hundreds, maybe thousands. And everything changed.

'Since then we have been attacking, not defending. We are driving them from Rojava, soon we will drive them from all the lands they have conquered and liberate the people that they enslaved.'

I was very surprised to hear such an admission. Up until then I had heard the spiel that had been drilled into the SDF fighters, that the defeats inflicted on Daesh were due to the superiority of the YPG and then, later, the SDF. That their tactics were the envy of the world and our fighters the best that could be. It was a line that caused all the foreigners to roll their eyes or else, when they had really had enough, to loudly point out that these tactics were extremely limited and responsible for many unnecessary casualties. It was apparent, from this admission, that at least one Kurd who had been through those battles of survival appreciated the failings in their system and how critical was the support of the outside world to the continued success of the autonomous region that was forming in northern Syria. It also gave me the opportunity to raise something that had been concerning me.

'We need to think about what happens when Daesh figure how to counter our airpower,' I said.

'They are not stupid, they will be working on this and if they can negate our support then we have to fight with ground forces only. And that means we need to improve our training and tactics, because at the moment we would not be able to do this. We don't have enough soldiers or equipment so we have to be able to use what we do have much better.'

He shrugged and looked unhappy.

'You're right,' he said, 'but we are not the generals or politicians. We fight as we know and do as we're told.'

'Fair enough,' I replied. 'But don't expect me to die through someone else's stupidity.'

That Daesh were learning lessons fast became more apparent as the days went on. As winter fully arrived heavy clouds suddenly formed and rain became routine, making our living outdoors a thoroughly miserable experience as we struggled to stay warm and dry. It also made the aircraft much more visible as they began to fly lower to support us, and that enabled Daesh to anticipate the threat they posed. On one occasion we were mortared repeatedly by an enterprising soul who'd set up his weapon in a house with some sort of movable roof. I watched as two F-15s circled for hours trying to locate him, but our crafty foe would time his shots perfectly so that the bombs launched when the planes were not in position to see. The Eagles tried various approaches, splitting up and coming in at different directions and times to try to spot the weapon firing, but all in vain. Eventually another pair of aircraft joined in, but still that mortar would hit us as soon as he got a break in their coverage. At last the planes gave up and left, and the mortar team happily dropped clusters of bombs all over us for the rest of the day. Their luck ran out the next day, when a mistimed firing was spotted by a roving fighter bomber and they were obliterated.

We hit a major Daesh position on 10 November and there followed a hell of a slugging match before we could clear them out. I couldn't appreciate it at the time, but this was the last major fight of the campaign. I was also to get a great surprise later when I met some new friends. We were billeted in a large abandoned village with the tanks and dushkas of the heavy weapons unit. I was returning from a mission, rifle slung on shoulder, looking forward to warming up around the campfire and getting some of the hot, teeth-achingly sweet tea that is a staple in the region, when a strange whirring noise caught my attention. I looked up, and was all but face to face with a large quadcopter that was descending on us.

'Drone!' I roared, unslinging my rifle and raising it. The drone was so close there was no question of me missing, except for the YPJ fighter who grabbed my arm.

'No, friend, friend,' she shouted.

This confused me. I was sure we had no such equipment, but as the drone landed I naturally went to investigate. I found a crowd of SDF standing around, as though spectating a sporting event, watching a team of obvious foreigners. Why obvious? They were dressed in the best uniforms I had seen, and which, though in SDF digital camouflage, were obviously Western-made. Their weapons were brand new Kalashnikovs with a whole host of rails and attachments, and they were either clean shaven or sporting long beards. Long beards were generally avoided by the SDF, as they were an affectation of

Daesh and having one made the likelihood of an accidental blue-on-blue in combat much higher. I myself had grown a bristling moustache (a source of great admiration among the Kurds) and attempted to blend in as much as possible in my choice of clothing – there's no point standing out in the crowd when Daesh snipers might be operating. One other giveaway was that though they all sported YPG shoulder flashes, one had evidently traded his in for a YPJ badge. The women fighters might respect a bit of male solidarity, but this was the YPG equivalent of wearing a burka.

Pushing my way through the crowd, I was able to listen in on the foreigners' conversation. They were French, and attached to us to provide live reconnaissance and forward control for airstrikes. I exchanged a few words with them in my schoolboy French and then left them alone. These soldiers were, naturally, very contained guys who were used to secrecy. In Rojava they suddenly found themselves being confronted with people from the West, often from their own countries (on occasion they even knew some of those people, in the case of former soldiers) and civilians at that. They were, as a result, extremely reserved with the foreign volunteers. However, they would in fairly short order be asking the volunteers, who tended to have a much better understanding of Kurdish and the culture, for help in dealing with the problems they were encountering. And we, in turn, were delighted to help, especially if it meant getting our paws on the rations that they were happy to share with us. By the time I left Syria, seeing the French guys would be just like meeting up with any other of the foreign crews that were in the tabors, with the added bonus that you'd get a decent cup of coffee.

The rise in the number of supportive airstrikes meant that Daesh wouldn't be able to hold us and, though there were a number of occasions where we met resistance, it was apparent that the campaign would soon be over. On 12 November we cleared the road between Hasakah and Tel Hamis, a major artery that had been closed for three years, while the next day we received the news that Shingal, where the Yazidis had been massacred and a bitter battle for control had been raging, had fallen to a combined Peshmerga/YPG force. On the evening of the 14th we heard that the other battle group had taken Al Hawl with few problems; Daesh's main resistance had been set to oppose our advance and they had rolled right over the enemy into the town in two weeks.

Daesh set to, salvaging what they could from the situation, and all across the area their fighters fled before we could complete our encirclement. This would prove a forlorn hope for many of them, as I was to see all too clearly.

On 15 November I was assigned to support a tabor that was to storm an oil facility up in the hills outside Al Hawl. To get there I had my first experience in one of the ancient MTLB armoured personnel carriers. These are designed to hold eleven passengers, but the YPG only had the merest handful of these precious vehicles and so we squeezed at least fifteen into the back. It was, to put it mildly, quite worrying. I was up at the front of the passenger compartment and had to sit on what turned out to be the fuel tank. Old Soviet armoured vehicles have a bad reputation for burning when hit, and Daesh had demonstrated their anti-tank missiles a few days previously when they had knocked out one of our dushkas. Things got worse when, after we had been squashed into the damn thing, the crew needed a hammer to close the one functioning hatch. Suddenly being on top of the fuel tank seemed like a good option: if we were hit, I would get burned up quicker than everyone else.

Needless to say, the trip across country to our assault point was unpleasant. But thankfully we arrived without exploding in blazing death. We then had the joy of sitting still and stuck while the crewman got out and applied his hammer to open the hatch. That was truly terrifying, waiting, trapped, not knowing if this was a defended position or if an RPG or missile was about to burst among us; cursing the crewman as he banged away on the hatch, making the whole vehicle ring like a giant bell; and all the time having the muzzle of someone's weapon stuck firmly against your backside and hoping to God that the safety was on because you could guarantee that it had a bullet chambered.

It was not nice, is the point I'm trying to make.

We moved into the facility with the SDF fire teams showing good discipline and covering each other as they took turns to leapfrog forwards. As snipers, we were to provide an additional layer of cover, acting as marksmen and observers against potential threats. There was nothing. Daesh had abandoned the place, and though we had to be watchful for the ever-present danger of mines, we were able to set up positions on the edge of the facility, which, as it overlooked the long valley that held the major populated areas, allowed us to keep an eye on the situation as the SDF cleared the locale.

My job was to guard our flank. A small village was at the top of the rise, about six hundred metres from us. As most of it stood on the other side of the slope we couldn't see what was happening and so it needed watching in case Daesh tried something from there. It didn't take long before I spotted activity.

'Got something,' I called to my partner sniper.

A couple of heads had peeped over the crest and regarded us. Soon more heads appeared and, after looking us over, what I imagine was some sort of village meeting started. Though most of the figures stayed obscured, a number, emboldened by the fact they weren't shot on sight, I'd guess, moved closer to get a better view of what was happening. More discussion – now with arm-waving – took place.

'Getting a lot of activity,' I reported.

'Keep watching. If they come towards us or you see a vehicle let me know.'

The meeting had evidently come to a decision.

'Christ! Motorbike coming!' I shouted the warning.

One of the ubiquitous 125cc bikes, which were the primary mode of transport in this part of the world, had come trundling up the road and pulled up in front of one of the few houses I had a clear view of. The driver was, quite obviously, Daesh. He had the long beard and was dressed in black. Through my scope he moved with the assurance of someone with authority. He was joined by two younger men, again with the classic look of the enemy, who stared at us across the distance for a period. Even at this range I could see the dark looks they were giving us through my scope. These guys were definite players.

'We got some. Sure they're Daesh,' I called out, clicked my safety off and settled. I could shoot the moment I needed to.

'Do they have weapons? We can't shoot unless they are armed or come at us,' I was told.

The men walked over to the bike and all three mounted. It was the most perfect target I would ever see. They were side on to me at six hundred metres, crammed onto the small bike, in front of a mud house that would stop any round I fired and therefore prevent any danger to bystanders behind my line of fire. With the Dragunov, at this range, I could kill all three in less than two seconds with three rapid shots. It was a dream.

But they weren't armed.

The bike started up and gurgled away back over the hill. With a curse I clicked my safety back on. But the rules were the rules and the rules were completely right. Shooting unarmed people, even if you do think they are the enemy, is fundamentally wrong. This was something that I would cling to in the future when the war became more intense.

It didn't help when one of our intelligence agents went over to the village ten minutes later and returned telling us that yes, they had been Daesh, and that the villagers were very happy that we had driven them away.

'Bollocks,' I said to myself, but there would be a ray of sunshine from this situation.

We radioed the news in to command, and shortly thereafter were told that other units were making similar reports. All across the battle zone Daesh troops were abandoning their weapons and getting picked up by motorbikes and pulling out. The Americans reported that their aerial recon showed bikes zipping all over the place, and told us they would monitor the situation.

As the day wore on this led to another rant at me about how the Americans weren't bombing the motorbikes, that they were letting Daesh get away, even that the Americans *wanted* Daesh to get away so that the SDF would sustain more casualties fighting them at a later date. I eventually snapped and told the fighter saying it that he was acting like a child and should be quiet and patient. I suspected I knew what the Americans were planning, and I was proved right. Late in the afternoon a single bomb fell at the far end of the valley and obliterated a building. It was out of our view but we heard the explosion clearly. Five minutes later the report came in. Daesh had been pulling their people back to a single point and the Americans, from their high perches, had watched them. Once they were sure that they were all gathered in one place, it was a simple matter to drop one bomb from an ever-circling B-1B. Job done.

Though Daesh were without doubt finished in this campaign – and knew it – they still managed to pull a few surprises, especially with their suicide vehicles. On the 18th I wandered back to my billet to find one of the armoured Hummers being dragged up in a really sorry state. The back of it had been blown clean off, though the tough armour had protected the crew compartment. Sitting drinking tea with the guys and girls from my tabor were my two friends Del Gesh and Kemal, who'd been crewing the vehicle. Kemal was his usual phlegmatic self (I reckon you'd have to throw Inbred out of a plane without a parachute before he'd start to worry), but Del Gesh was evidently in shock, shaking uncontrollably. They'd been on a casualty evacuation mission when a VBIED had attacked them. The Hummer driver had run the vehicle for all it was worth and the suicide bomber had chased them down. Kemal had been inside the vehicle but Del Gesh was crewing the machine gun in the open turret. He had poured fire into their pursuer, but against such a target such efforts are futile and the VBIED had slowly closed the distance on them. Then, at a mere fifteen metres, the VBIED ran over a mine that they had miraculously missed.

I've talked about the size of the explosions that these weapons make. It was incredible that they hadn't been killed, and that realisation was obviously what was hitting Del Gesh. He'd seen death about as up close as you can and still walk away.

There was one last town to be taken to complete the op, and we attacked on 18 November. It was a sizeable settlement on the shore of a large lake, and we didn't know what to expect. I wasn't part of the assault unit; my job was to watch from a berm two kilometres outside the edge of town for any movement. It was quickly apparent that the whole place was deserted, but prior to the attack the SDF did their usual preparatory bombardment with dushkas and, to my delight, a tank. Though I'd spent a lot of time around these things in our laagers and knew the crews well, I had never had the chance to see the SDF use them in action. So it was with great interest that I watched the big beast, an ancient T-55 that had previously belonged to the Syrian army, rumble up beside me at the berm. The crew carefully aimed the cannon and then decamped from the turret, running a length of string behind them. I was confused, but would soon find out that this was a standard practice with the SDF, who didn't have any faith in the gun breech on the old tanks and always fired them from outside the vehicle via a lanyard. With a lot of shouting and waving of arms to let everyone know that they were about to fire, the gunner, almost with an air of ceremony, yanked on the cord.

The blast was, as to be expected, impressive, and I turned to see where the shell hit. I didn't know what they were firing at, but thought that anything deserving one of our rare and precious tank shells would be worth keeping an eye on, in case Daesh suddenly spilt out of it. But there was nothing to see. The shell, I assumed, was a dud.

The lack of reaction caused a lot more shouting and head scratching, and the crew remounted and reloaded, readjusted the cannon, again climbed out of the roof hatches trailing their length of string and got set for another shot. Not wanting to miss anything, I set the video on my phone running.

Again, the great blast followed by nothing. Despite this, the crew declaimed loudly that it was mission accomplished and heaved their monster away from the rest of us and back to the rear. One of the French Special Forces guys, who had been watching among the large crowd of spectators, wandered over to me.

'What were they shooting at?' he enquired.

'I've no idea,' I replied, and settled down to watch the footage.

The first two reviews showed nothing that I could make out, but the third was the charm and I spotted the shell fall. It had hit less than a kilometre away, in the fields between us and the edge of town, and had then skipped like a skimming stone across the dirt. As the soil was now damp from the regular rain it didn't throw up much of a dust cloud, so it was easy to miss. I would have told the tank boys about it but they'd left already and I don't suppose they'd have appreciated me pointing out how terrible their shooting had been.

I subsequently found out that this particular tank had had its sights smashed and the crew aimed by staring straight down the gun barrel at whatever it was they wanted to shoot. Regardless, I still think it was quite remarkable. The T-55 might be ancient, but to miss an entire town – come on!

The town was the last possible position for Daesh, and was taken in a few hours. The next day we were told we would be heading back to Sari Kani. I learnt that we had recovered some 450 dead Daesh during the operation, but that their casualties would almost certainly be heavier as many would have been blown literally to pieces or else buried under rubble from the bombing. Our casualties had been extremely light in comparison, and the first operation of the SDF could be regarded as a resounding success.

7

Home by Christmas . . . Then Back Again

December/January 2015–16

The end of the Al Hawl campaign seemed like a good time to take a break from the war. I had spent almost six months in Iraq and Syria, and thought going home for Christmas and the New Year would be a good idea, both to reassure my family and friends that everything was fine and for myself. So I bade farewell to my friends in the sniper tabor and started the reverse journey back to the UK, which would require passing through KDP-controlled areas in Kurdistan and the threat of a month in jail if caught. Fortunately, this didn't happen: the trip to Erbil, where I would fly from, went smoothly. I knew that I would be back in the New Year, so booked my return ticket while waiting for our contact to arrange our flights home.

There were a number of other volunteers heading to their

respective homes, many with the same agenda as me, and we made the most of being in the modern city. In short, we made gluttons of ourselves, a term I hadn't really understood until I stood in an Erbil restaurant with a skinny Frenchman who ordered an entire pizza and two different burger meals because he couldn't decide what he wanted – and then watched him eat the lot! We also made up on our enforced abstinence from alcohol with a vengeance. This prohibition meant our tolerance to booze was now extremely low, which made for much cheaper nights – which was fortunate as we were all running on almost no money.

The financial situation was particularly serious for the guys who had failed to meet the terms of their contract with the YPG, having not undertaken the six months' service required. This meant that the Kurds did not feel obligated to pay their visa costs and air fares home. There was some leeway (for example, I had completed about five and a half months, but my good record with the Kurds smoothed the way), but those who were badly short in completing their terms or had a reputation for being *no boş* would have to pay their own way. As every volunteer had already laid out considerable personal funds just to get to Iraq, those who had to get themselves home too would normally be looking for the cheapest way to travel. And that meant flying with Turkish Airways, generally via Istanbul or Ankara.

One of the volunteers who tried this was a Norwegian who, though he had been into Rojava twice, was leaving only three months into his second stint. He had fought throughout the Al Hawl operation but did not wish to sit around waiting for another campaign to start; this was a standard method for some of the guys, who'd fly back when word came through that another op was in preparation. As he was broke he decided to try his chances with a cheap flight through Turkey, despite many of us warning him of our misgivings. He was known as a YPG fighter in his own country and had given interviews there in between trips, and was wise enough to inform the Norwegian consulate in Erbil of his travel plans before flying. He said goodbye to us, went to the airport, and caught his flight. And vanished.

Three days later he reappeared in Erbil, having been deported from Turkey. All of the volunteers waiting to leave had become deeply concerned and it was with great relief that we welcomed him back. He was suffering from shock, and was deaf in one ear from where he had taken a beating. He told us he had been pulled out of the queue while going through the transit security check and taken to a facility in a basement in another building. There he was held for three days without charge. He was refused access to his embassy, suffered deliberate sleep deprivation, was interrogated and beaten. He was accused of being first a Kurdish agent, and then a Russian one. He was of the opinion that he was only spared worse treatment because he warned his interrogators that he was going to respond to further violence with his own, and that they would have to kill him. As his government knew he was transiting through Turkey, this would cause diplomatic issues. He said that what really scared him was the sound of screaming from elsewhere in the facility, which went on for almost the entire time he was incarcerated. It was not a place any person would ever want to go, and he no doubt got away much lighter than many others.

The YPG, to their credit, put him up and arranged his flight back to Norway.

The next day it was my turn to fly, and I nearly screwed it up royally.

Security in Erbil airport is exceptionally tight, which is fair enough when you consider how close Daesh territory is to the city and that it is the capital of Iraqi Kurdistan and the main stronghold of the KDP. You can't actually drive straight to the airport; all vehicles have to go through a security checkpoint, where they are checked by armed guards and sniffer dogs. You then take a bus to the terminal, where you go through security at the door, including passing through metal and bomb detectors, and your baggage goes through a brand-new X-ray machine, all before you enter the building.

When my rucksack set off an alarm I was not really surprised. I thought I might be in line for some sort of shakedown. Two polite, but armed, guards asked me to empty the contents and began to rummage through them. This was alarming as my YPG uniform was squashed into the bottom of the bag and, considering the antipathy that existed between the KDP and the YPG, I was not keen on it coming to light.

'Perhaps you could tell me what you are after?' I asked, hoping to avoid literally airing my dirty laundry.

'There is something here that is not allowed,' the guard answered.

'Ah. I think I know what it is,' I exclaimed, and dug out a zip case that contained a number of expended shell cases which I had gathered up over the months. I had intended them to be gifts for the children of family and friends, which may seem a bit weird, but most kids seem to love them. Besides, it was a cheap Christmas present and shopping opportunities had been thin on the ground.

'No. These are not allowed, but there is something else,' he said.

I was slightly mystified, but the light dawned as I pulled a black plastic bag from the depths of my pack. Months before, when I had been enjoying the balmy days on the banks of the Euphrates, one of my ancient and decrepit Kalashnikov magazines had proved itself so rotten and unreliable that I had discarded it. I had thrown the thirty bullets it contained into a black plastic bag and stowed it in my kit, intending to load the bullets into another magazine when I needed to. And had then proceeded to forget all about them.

'Oh SHIT!'

I can only say that it came out as a yelp, and evidently was so funny that the two guards actually cracked up. One of them took the bag of ammunition from me and tipped it out into a tray for examination. Lots of brass glittered in the light.

'You know that these are not allowed, yes?'

'I'm so sorry, I forgot they were there!'

'You were a soldier? You were fighting?'

'Yes . . . (time to make a decision) I was with YPG . . . in Syria.'

'OK. You have uniform? Prove you not Daesh?'

I dug out my tatty, smelly uniform jacket. The bright yellow of the YPG shoulder flash was plain to see.

'OK. This is no problem. But you cannot take the bullets. Big problem for plane and your country, yes?'

'Yes. Thank you for finding them.'

'No problem. Thank you for coming and fighting for us.'

And I flew home.

This may seem ludicrous – and it was – but I was lucky it hadn't been a grenade. At that stage of the war in Syria, we tended to accrue ordnance because you could never be sure when you could reliably get more.

This situation demonstrated how, though the Kurdish political parties might detest each other, the average Kurd was inclined to view those who came from abroad to fight – even for another group – highly favourably. To their mind, we were there for all of their people and were touched that foreigners would come and fight their enemy on their behalf. This attitude well and truly saved me from what could have been a disaster of my own carelessness.

I had no problems with UK passport control as officialdom was still getting its collective head around the issue of foreign volunteers. At the desk I was asked what I had been doing in Iraq for the last six months.

'I wasn't,' I replied. 'I was in Syria fighting against ISIS.' I didn't see the point in lying. If there was going to be an issue it would only be more complicated if I wasn't honest.

The immigration officer didn't quite know what to make of that, and turned to regard a man in a suit standing behind the consoles watching us. He inclined his head slightly and I was stamped through.

'Welcome home,' I was told. 'And good on you.'

Back in the UK, the gluttony continued unabated. I had my return flight already booked and wanted to make the most of the time I had, so travelled all over the place catching up with family and friends. All wanted to know about what had happened, what I had been doing, and said 'proud of you' with that tone of 'mad bastard', but it was a great time and all understood my drive to go back.

I also used the time to get equipment that would be useful for when I returned, as my time in Rojava had shown me that the basic-issue SDF webbing and uniforms were – though functional – not of great quality. As I was returning to the snipers I could take certain items back both for my own efficiency and for the guys in the unit: two new uniforms, one thick for the winter campaigning and a lightweight one for the summer; an assault vest that would allow me to carry all of my mission equipment and ammunition instead of having to rely on a day sack; and a Russian military surplus bipod for a Dragunov. I purchased a number of bore-snakes, which allow one to quickly clean a rifle barrel – one for me, the rest for the unit. I bought two other pieces of equipment that experience had taught me would be invaluable: a small fold-away solar panel for keeping phones charged (a decent phone is a tremendous piece of equipment – camera, word processor and communications all in one handy device) and a pair of Howard Leight active ear protectors. These allowed me to hear clearly (in fact, they enhanced my hearing quite a lot, which was very useful on night guard or patrols) but shut down instantly when a loud noise occurred, such as when shooting or if an explosion went off near by. I'm sure any remaining hearing I have is entirely down to these fantastic protectors, especially considering how loud things would get in the following months. I also stocked up on medical equipment, with the emphasis on immediate trauma treatment. Blood-clotting agents, tourniquets and combat dressings would make up a fair part of my personal combat load from now on.

I was quite busy in the six weeks I was in the UK and the time flew by. There was a couple of days talking to the authorities, in the shape of Special Branch and a team from the Ministry of Defence, who called me out of the blue and were very interested in the situation in Syria. We spent hours discussing my observations on what was happening. I was glad to help as I viewed the war on ISIS as a group effort. Division and subterfuge between allies would only benefit the enemy, and as I had been writing reports on the situation for various journalists, politicians and activists while I had been in Syria, and planned to carry on doing so when I returned, it was no problem to assure these agencies that I would keep them in the loop. I was also asked to be on the lookout for any material that might be useful in providing information on Daesh activities and personnel, particularly British citizens, something I was happy to do.

Meanwhile in Syria the SDF continued their successes. Throughout December and January they engaged in a major operation to storm the Tishrin dam, a critical strategic crossing point of the Euphrates south of Sarrin. The operation was a great success – the SDF took the dam and then launched a rapid encirclement that completely routed local Daesh forces and took thirty kilometres of ISIS territory. More than one hundred villages were liberated and the SDF were able to seize substantial quantities of weapons, including two tanks and a BMP armoured infantry carrier. I'm sorry I missed it, as it was a great success in the war against Daesh and when I arrived back at the sniper tabor, via the usual trip through northern Iraq and across the border, on 24 January my friends regaled me with their stories of the offensive.

Another major development had occurred. The Americans had begun building an airstrip outside Hasakah and we would now start to see much greater quantities of supplies and equipment coming in to bulk up the SDF inventory. We would be able to plan and prepare for much larger operations as we no longer had to rely on ancient weapon stashes or weapons smugglers. I wasn't aware of how much support we would receive and this led me to propose something that I had been contemplating in my time away.

Both my experience in Al Hawl and that of the men and women of my unit in Tishrin indicated that Daesh were using VBIEDs as a primary weapon against us. These could be kept hidden until the last moment and then sprung in ambush, meaning units under attack had to rely only on their personal weapons to deal with them. Stopping these armoured beasts could be extremely difficult, and even if they failed to kill many victims VBIEDs were very effective at creating holes in defences which could then be exploited by follow-on attacks by infantry.

As the YPG had minimal anti-tank weapons and RPGs have far too short an effective range to stop VBIEDs (if you can even hit them – RPGs require a lot of either training and skill or luck to be effective against a fast-moving target) I suggested a possible counter. The YPG's very heavy sniper rifles were at that time sitting in armouries as they are too heavy for mobile operations. While greatly valued for their sheer power, the Şer were too difficult for sniper teams to use effectively, except from defensive positions. My idea was that instead of the sniper teams using them, the Şer could be issued to standard infantry units as an anti-VBIED measure. With a simple peep metal sight they would provide an effective weapon out to around five hundred metres. The fact that the Şer's 14.5mm bullet, which is a real monster, had originally been designed for knocking out tanks early in the Second World War meant it would prove very effective against the sort of armour that the VBIEDs were being fitted with.

This was met with some interest and I was advised to write to high command with the idea, but back came the response that the problem was well in hand and that the SDF had the means to deal with the VBIED threat. I was slightly confused by this reaction, as my proposal made use of a readily available and unused resource, but put it down to the stubbornness that the locals had to ideas coming from outsiders. It turned out to be ingenuous of me, as in a few weeks I would find out the reason for the SDF's confidence in their capabilities.

8

Shaddadi and Onwards

February/March 2016

I'd timed my return well. The snipers were engaged in their standard pre-operation training regime, which entailed ideological training and discussion groups interspersed with some shooting practice, though ammunition was still limited. After their successes in Al Hawl and at the Tishrin dam all of the SDF troops were extremely confident. Knowing that another attack was imminent filled all of us with excitement.

On 16 February we launched a night assault over the Abdul Aziz mountains, heading south across the plains to our target, the town of Shaddadi. It was while waiting in camp for the signal to start the attack that I had the opportunity to meet some of the new allies that were coming to join the SDF alliance. I was sitting with a Kurdish SDF tabor when a number of brand-new luxury 4 × 4s pulled up to our camp and out stepped an Arab sheik, the leader of the local tribe. And his bodyguard.

You could cut the tension with a knife, and I saw many of the SDF glance over to their stacked weapons. The bodyguards wore a rag-tag assortment of military equipment, though all new and in good condition, sported curly beards and tucked their trousers into their socks. Not to put too fine a point on it, but had I been looking at them through my scope I would have pulled the trigger. They looked like Daesh, because up until recently that's what they had been. This illustrated the situation of the local Arabs rather well, and indeed of all the various ethnic groups in the myriad factions fighting each other in the Syrian Civil War. If a particular group took control of your home you could: 1) fight them; 2) run away; 3) accept it and make the correct salute to their fighters when they passed.*

The sheik had allied with Daesh when they took control of the region. I can't blame him: he had his people to think about and the terror tactics that Daesh employed meant that plenty of people would simply concede power to them to avoid their wrath. Ever the pragmatist, when he had seen that the writing was on the wall for ISIS he switched allegiance to the SDF. No doubt his men's beards would soon be trimmed and the uniforms switched to the standard SDF pattern, but at that moment, face to face with men who would have been our enemies weeks (perhaps even days) before, it was somewhat disconcerting.

* This was particularly amusing when it involved small children. Used to giving the single-fingered Daesh salute for years to passing fighters they'd excitedly do the same to SDF when they first caught sight of our columns passing through, only to have parents dive on them and make them do the two-fingered SDF sign (as the Western 'peace' sign). SDF troopers never took exception to this and always found it funny.

The same could be said for them, but as the sheik was keen to prove that he was now a committed and reliable friend, he made a point of shaking the hand of every soldier gathered there. Evidently a true diplomat, he barely baulked when the women fighters joined the queue and made great play of pumping his hand vigorously and addressing him directly, something that under Daesh rule would have been utterly unthinkable. But he made his point that he, and his tribe, were on our side and departed to perform the ritual with the other units camped in the mountains, waiting to launch our attack.

A few hours later the assault began, and it was clear that Daesh once again seemed to have been caught by surprise. We captured our first day's objective by noon. The main resistance was a suicide car attack that achieved nothing but the killing of five civilians. I stood and watched as the men of the tiny hamlet dug holes in the rock-hard ground to bury two children who had been killed by the explosion while their women screamed their grief. It was truly horrible and it occurred to me that if we hadn't come here these children would still be alive. But we had, and they were dead. And it isn't right or fair that those innocents should die, but that is the way it is. You either fight and accept the consequences, or else accept the authority of those who are willing to use violence. I would hope that if you are fighting for the right reasons, then in the long term the people will benefit from peace and just government. But that doesn't make the toll any less hard to bear.

VBIEDs were apparently going to prove a major threat in this campaign, and I thought it prudent to double check the measures for our defence when we stopped for the night. A number of units had settled into a large village and among them were foreign volunteers. As was usual in such circumstances, we would tend to come together to exchange news and shoot the breeze. I asked if anyone knew whether mines had been placed to thwart a potential night attack by any VBIEDs in the area, only to receive some surprising news.

'Nah,' one of the American volunteers told me. 'They've got a Javelin up there,' and nodded towards a knoll that stood beside the village.

I admit, I scoffed. A Javelin? One of the most advanced anti-tank missile systems in the world, and I was expected to believe that we had got our hands on one? Surely it was one of the ancient Milans that you occasionally saw rattling around on operations.

'Whatever, dude,' he shrugged. 'That's what they told me they had.'

I didn't believe him, so I wandered up the hill and to my astonishment there were two SDF troopers, accompanied by a couple of French Special Forces, scanning the surrounding terrain through the thermal scope of a Javelin missile.

One of my fellow snipers came up.

'You should not be here,' he said, and tugged my arm to take me away.

'That's a Javelin!'

'Yes, but it's a secret so come away.'

'But that's a fucking Javelin!'

'Yes, shush, come away. And don't swear.'

The reason for the SDF's confidence in dealing with VBIEDs was now plain. A fire-and-forget weapon with state-of-the-art sights, the Javelin would prove a ferocious killer of suicide vehicles and was a quantum leap in capability. Unfortunately, the limited number of systems in theatre meant that they couldn't be everywhere, and we still had to rely on other measures to protect ourselves from the threat.

The next evening, I was just drifting off to sleep when the alarm sounded. Cursing and rushing out into the dark to find out what was going on, I was treated to the sight of a huge explosion and fireball rising into the sky perhaps a kilometre away. A suicide car had made to attack us but had hit a mine that our sabotage teams had laid for this very purpose. I can't be sure, but I think the car had been intended to soften up our defences before an attack, as an AC-130 gunship then turned up and proceeded to comprehensively blast something just out of sight.

We continued a breakneck advance and 19 February would see me supporting a tabor a few kilometres outside Shaddadi. We rushed through neighbourhoods at such speed that many civilians were caught by surprise; the first they knew that the SDF were so close was when we tore past them looking for Daesh. The strategy was risky, as we had to treat civilians with caution: Daesh were still using their favourite tactic of approaching us disguised as harmless civilians before detonating a suicide vest. However, we also wanted to win the support of the residents and the only way to do this was to engage with them.

We had pushed forward in an armoured carrier and launched the clearance operation of a suburb of Shaddadi. I was assigned to protect the tabor commander and overwatch with a scoped M16. The clearance was proceeding well when we became aware of a disturbance in the field behind the command point. Two women, burdened with huge loads and half a dozen small children, were trying to hurry away across the fields and, because of their cargoes, making only a snail's pace. Even from a distance of two hundred metres we could see the sheer terror on their faces as they glanced over at us and tried to make their escape.

The commander, a woman of perhaps only twenty-five, watched them with a furrowed brow before signalling for me to come with her as she worked out what exactly was going on. We walked across the field towards the women, taking care to scan all around as it was possible this was some sort of trap and we were walking into someone's crosshairs, but their reaction became more extreme. They began to shriek in terror and tried to drag their children – who watched us with wide-eyed fear – along quicker. If it was a trap it was one designed to set the target at maximum alert.

We soon caught up with them and the commander asked them, in Arabic, what was the matter. The answer was even more screams, interspersed with appeals for mercy. The whole situation seemed to be descending into chaos, and I was put even more on edge when an elderly man approached us. It was looking more and more like a threatening situation, and we ordered him to stop and stay back. He in turn began, with great dignity, to calmly ask us to have pity on the women and children, who continued to wail and stagger away from us.

This, regardless to say, caused some confusion for the commander and me. She asked them what he was talking about, and learned that Daesh had told them that the atheist PKK was coming and were going to kill all the Arabs in the district. The commander and I exchanged an incredulous look.

'We are not PKK. And why would we kill you? We are here to liberate you,' she assured him. 'Do you need food or cigarettes? Come over here, we have supplies we can share with you.'

The look on his face when he realised we were not simply toying with him and meant what we were saying was indescribable. He clasped his hands together and, voice breaking, thanked God. I had just witnessed one of the greatest examples of bravery that I would ever see. Seeing two soldiers whom he thought were committed to murder cross over to the fleeing women and their children, the old man, evidently one of the local leaders, had come to try to save them, even though he had known it might cost him his own life. Realising that there was no truth in what they had been told about our motives, the group followed us over to our supply dump and, after the children had been thoroughly fussed over by the troopers, left laden down with goodies. Of course, this soon meant that civilians starting flocking in, looking for free food and, most especially prized, cigarettes. I can safely say that the banning of smoking by ISIS was one of our greatest assets for winning over the locals.

The violation of the no-smoking rule could have severe consequences, as could a number of other 'crimes'. Our new friends in the village became quite chatty and one man told me how he had received forty lashes from Daesh, twenty for smoking and twenty for having a tattoo. The villagers also gave us intelligence that Daesh had fled before our advance and had dug in at the school and the hospital in the town.

Our advance saw us on the outskirts of Shaddadi by the 20th and a major position was prepared on the main road, two kilometres outside the town.* A berm was built to provide cover from fire and to stop car bombs from coming straight in among us, and we were joined by a French/SDF Javelin team and a swarm of American Special Forces, who rolled up in a column of heavily armed vehicles that looked like they'd been stolen off the set of a *Mad Max* movie. I was pleased to see them, as it looked like we were going to enjoy the full support of the United States in this war, which would make things considerably easier.

The position also hosted the full gamut of the SDF's firepower, which was arrayed to undertake a preparatory bombardment of the edge of the town prior to our assault. Dozens of dushkas of various calibres were joined by a tank, and even a Katyusha rocket launcher and a recoilless rifle mounted on the back of a pick-up. It would be the first time I saw these two weapons in action with the SDF, and they were to prove a bit of a disappointment. The recoilless rifle team set itself up and several hundred interested SDF stood around to watch. With great aplomb the weapon was fired – only for the shell to land a hundred metres in front of us. A collective snigger went up and the crew, looking flustered, reset their aim for a second shot. This landed about halfway between us and the town, and I experienced a sensation of déjà vu as I was reminded of the tank in the Al Hawl operation that had bounced its shells across the field. This got even stronger when the Katyusha began to add its fire, which resulted in rockets corkscrewing all over the place leaving

* For some reason the YPG released that they took Shaddadi on 19 February. That is categorically not the case: the heaviest fighting was yet to come.

smoky contrails behind them. An American Special Forces soldier dropped down beside me on the berm and asked me:

'Hey bro, you know what they're shooting at?'

'Whatever they hit, I suspect,' I said.

This would prove true a moment later, when one of the rockets spiralled across the sky and struck a warehouse on the edge of the town. A cheer went up and the crew, honour satisfied, withdrew.

It may seem that I am giving the SDF a hard time for the accuracy of their heavy weapons, so I will point out that, considering the issues the SDF were facing at this time, it is actually quite understandable. If there was limited ammunition available for training on small arms then there was none available for the crews of these weapons. The only opportunity they had to fire the weapons was in action, and even in combat there was scant ammunition.

With the fire from the heavy weapons proving so ineffective, the dushkas had to provide our main barrage to soften up any suspected positions. This continued for the rest of the morning, but had just about petered out when a shout of alarm went up. A VBIED was tearing up the straight road out of Shaddadi towards us, the driver's foot flat on the floor. Dozens of soldiers started shooting with every weapon to hand, but the bullets simply pinged off the thick armour. I shot two rounds from my Dragunov, aiming at the driver's view port, but it was apparent that the bomb was going to hit us. I grabbed my rifle, rose and turned to run as far and as fast as I could to get away from the blast when a sudden *whoosh* and a bang told me that our attacker had met his match. At point-blank range the Javelin team had nailed the VBIED. I turned to see it rolling past us and away up the road, flames pouring from the stricken vehicle.

A great cheer went up as the vehicle rolled to a halt behind our position, where it promptly exploded with the now-expected towering fireball. Another cheer, and then someone screamed for everyone to take cover as the inevitable debris peppered us. But we were all very happy. Our new missile had proven to be lethal to this feared opponent and we knew that we now had a potent weapon at our disposal. Daesh seemed to take the hint as they didn't try any more attacks that afternoon.

The next day, a sandstorm blew up. I don't know if the SDF command decided to use this as cover for our assault or if it was simply scheduled then anyway, but we attacked from all points on the town through the howling dust. Heavy fighting ensued as our infantry advanced towards the centre of the town and the snipers were sent to try to assist. Only a limited number of our unit were allowed to move up to join the most forward units; I and most of my comrades had to settle for trying to provide cover from positions further back. I was given an unusual way of judging the range to the enemy when, while running across a roof to assume a position, I clearly saw an RPG shoot across right in front of me, about twenty metres away, before self-detonating. I knew that these rockets blew themselves up at about nine hundred metres, so I now had a good idea of the range. Unfortunately the wind continued to build, bringing more sand with it, and the visibility dropped. I could see SDF forces fighting fiercely in the streets against Daesh, but the conditions meant any shots taken at that range would have to be very carefully chosen so as to not risk friendly forces. I had to restrict myself to shooting at targets like large buildings that showed activity and, being unable to spot my fall of shot, I soon gave it up as a waste of time. The SDF fought on through the gathering dusk and gradually drove Daesh out of most of the town, reducing them to a few key positions.

On the 22nd, another sniper and I were sent to look for a reported Daesh sniper who was thought to be in the hospital. We joined a tabor that had taken over a smashed building overlooking the hospital and main crossroads heading into Shaddadi. Across the road was a wooded area with houses behind it. Daesh had dug trenches in among the trees and we assumed that the houses were also fortified.

We knew straight away that we weren't dealing with a sniper. Our building was two storeys high and the staircase up from the ground floor to the roof, where the SDF made their positions, had been blasted open. It was directly exposed both to the elements and to the hospital and Daesh trenches. Soldiers were walking up and down it constantly in full view of any Daesh who may have been watching.

My partner and I exchanged a look, and he told the commander of the tabor we were supporting that there was no sniper there. She assured us that one of her men had just been missed by a bullet. It must be a sniper!

As diplomatically as we could, we explained that if a sniper had been operating there she would have lost half her command by now. I am no great marksman – I would rank myself as fair, especially with the Dragunov – but if I had been in that hospital with plenty of targets wandering around at five hundred metres with no cover, I'd have racked up a considerable number of kills without any real issues. We were, quite frankly, like ducks in a shooting gallery.

The position was truly awful. Apart from being perfect sniper bait, we suffered from the biting wind and rain on the roof. The building was also offset to the left of the crossroads, so instead of being able to see clearly down the straight road into the centre of town and spot any potential car bomb coming at a distance, the first notice we would get was when any vehicle approached the crossroads themselves, only about three or four hundred metres distant. I was very unhappy about the location and asked to be allowed to move, but this wasn't permitted.

We'd been given our job and so settled down into position to keep watch. I resolved that if for some reason I had to go downstairs, then it would be at a full sprint down each flight. Just because no sniper was operating currently, it didn't mean that wouldn't change rapidly. And the first thing we would know about it would be the gunshot.

Fortunately Daesh was on its last legs in Shaddadi, though we didn't know that at the time. On two occasions Daesh troops dashed across the road, once from the woods to the hospital and then back again a few hours later. Each time the soldiers in the tabor started yelling and jumping around, waving their arms. But as our location gave us such a limited view, the target would be across our sight range in three to four seconds, even if we'd been looking at the road instead of scanning the hospital windows and roof for the imaginary sniper.

My patience with this unit was already stretched when at 1800 they suddenly went nuts. The machine-gunner abruptly let rip – I never found out why – and the rest of the unit promptly rushed over and unloaded at the whole of creation. I scanned through my scope, seeking a target. Surely there was something out there.

Not only was there no target, there was nothing. No movement. No return fire. Nothing but our tracers lighting up the dusk.

It was when the RPG gunner ran up to the parapet and shot a rocket straight into the ground in front of us, about twenty metres away, that I decided I'd had enough of this anarchy. The noise of an RPG being fired is deafening, and when it happens a metre from your head, without warning, it is not dissimilar to a stun grenade. Even through my ear protectors the *CRACK* was painfully loud. Without them, my hearing would likely have been irreparably damaged. I took my rifle down and sat on the floor with my back to the parapet.

'Why aren't you firing?' demanded the squad commander, blasting away with her AK. As she did this while looking and talking at me, this sort of summed up the quality of these particular troops.

'No Daesh,' I said.

'Yes, yes, Daesh!' she screamed.

'No. No Daesh,' I replied, and cleaned my fingernails.

Gradually the firing slowed and stopped. The machine-gunner proudly claimed to have killed at least three Daesh. If you add up every kill claim made by the SDF there would be no one left in the Middle East.

I was (I'd say understandably) a bit nonplussed by how the day had panned out. We were obviously on a wild goose chase with a bunch of idiots and I was not happy. Fortunately, that evening I was given a bit of a boost by the Americans. With their banshee scream, two A-10s swept through the twilight and with their characteristic *BRRRRMMMMHH* the 30mm cannons started giving some poor saps in the middle of town a hard time. It might sound morbid, possibly psychopathic, but I loved that noise. Whenever you heard it, it perked you right up. It's the sort of noise gods make when they are angry.

Flitting like bats in the dark they continued to hammer away as a huge storm of small-arms fire started up in town. The sheer quantity of it made me suspect that the US Special Forces guys were getting the aggression out of their systems. This was confirmed when a Javelin suddenly shot up into the air and arced high and gracefully across the sky like a shooting star before knocking the top of a building off. The SDF didn't use their precious missiles on such targets; they didn't have enough to squander.

That cheered me up, but the next day there was an incident that not only confirmed that this unit was a real bunch of jokers, but also highlighted an issue that was all too common throughout the YPG. After pulling a six-hour watch, I slunk off to my sleeping bag at 2 a.m. Alas, it began to rain, and as no one thought to wake me so I could get under cover the water seeped through the bag and my clothes, and I woke up after two hours' sleep to find myself completely drenched. The temperature was barely above freezing and I realised that, with no change of clothing, soaking wet and with a howling wind dropping the effective temperature even more, I was in real danger of exposure.

The Kurds in the unit I was supporting had insisted we all

sleep on the roof (they had a shelter for themselves, which didn't have room for us attached snipers), but I figured I had no choice but to move downstairs into the ruined shell of the building to seek some shelter from the wind.

A room on the ground floor, which looked out onto the crossroads by the hospital, was the only place I could find with no whistling draught. I was shaking uncontrollably from the cold, and though I'd taken my clothes off and wrung them out as best I could my teeth were still chattering. A fire was out of the question until daybreak, so I scouted around for something to keep me warm.

What I found wasn't pleasant, but served its purpose well. When the building had been taken two Daesh had made a stand there and been killed. The YPG had dragged their bodies out and buried them around the back in shallow graves, but a blanket they'd used had been discarded inside the room I'd found. It was covered in dried gore and, despite the cold, stank like a slaughter yard. But it was dry and warm, and in such situations you are glad for what you can find.

I wrapped myself in the blood-matted wool and then stood and watched the road junction through the shattered wall. I had a bad feeling. The rain and cold had driven our sentries inside the scant shelter on the roof, and I knew from how this tabor worked that they would not be watching, but sleeping instead. And Daesh would probably draw the same conclusion. Who likes sitting out in the freezing rain and wind, after all? So I guessed that if Daesh were going to make a move it would be on this particular grim morning, and I was damned if I was going to get killed in my sleep because of my colleagues' incompetence. As it turned out my reading was correct, though thankfully not in the manner I'd expected.

As I have already said, I wasn't happy with the position we had been stuck with. We only had an effective view of the road out to three hundred metres, and in the event of a suicide vehicle attack that would not give us enough time either to knock out the attacker or flee the building. We were far too exposed. And I expected a suicide attack. So I stood and watched, my manky blanket wrapped around me, to insulate me and the Kalashnikov in my hands. The range was too close for the Dragunov, and I had a plan. As soon as any vehicle coming from the centre of town got into my line of sight, I would shoot off half a dozen rounds, at most, while screaming my lungs out, and then I was going to get the hell out of there. I could scoot out of my room, down the corridor and straight out the back through another blown-down wall. That would put me on flat ground with our building (which I assumed would be the target) between me and the bomb. And I would be accelerating rapidly away through the trees. I might just make it, if it wasn't too big an explosion.

It was just after 6 a.m. when the truck came.

I was exhausted, but at least I'd warmed up a bit, and was standing with my mind blank as I watched the drizzle. The vehicle appeared through the haze, approaching the crossroads. A detached part of my brain noted it was driving slowly, not the sudden rush I'd been anticipating. The rest of me was reacting.

I screamed 'ARABA!' – Kurmanji for car. The AK snapped up to my shoulder; the safety came off in the same movement. I had my target in the sights, which I'd pre-set to the correct range. I was about to deliver a heap of problems to someone. In such a situation your world narrows down to a sliver. There's the target, the sights, the feel of the blood in your head, the breath in your lungs. It is, in my experience, the most focused you can be, about to initiate fire upon an enemy, before the bullets start coming back. You squeeze the trigger. You can't miss.

click

'FUCK!' The first round, some ancient piece of junk that had probably been rattling around in every warzone since Vietnam and had been made God knows when, had misfired.

I racked the action to eject it and took aim again. The detached part of my brain monitoring the situation reported that the truck wasn't heading towards us, but had turned left to follow the road out of town. It also appeared to be unarmoured, and had fighters watching over the sides. This wasn't an attack. It was a breakout.

This had all taken place in less than four seconds.

As the truck started to pull away I laid into it with the Kalashnikov. Round after round punched into the vehicle and I could see the chaos among the men in the back. Some were trying to take cover while others were trying to figure where the fire was coming from, in order to return it. The truck accelerated hard, knocking all of them around like skittles.

I emptied that first mag, even on single shot and gradually adjusting my fire for the increasing range, within ten seconds. Then I spun around and ran to the turn in the staircase, which had been blown open and from where I would be able to keep sight of the target for longer. As I went up the stairs three at a time I slammed a fresh magazine into the rifle and twitched the sights up to five hundred metres. I reached the hole (more accurately described as a complete absence of wall) and snapped three more rounds at the rapidly disappearing truck.

'Why you shoot? Why you shoot?' the YPJ squad commander was shouting at me from the floor above. I turned and looked up at her. My face told everything about my feelings and she actually took a step back.

'There was a fucking truck. If that'd been an attack, we'd be fucking dead,' I said in English. She didn't understand anything apart from the 'fucking', but she knew damn well that I was royally pissed off.

Switching to Kurdish I said, 'If car bomb – we dead,' and stalked back downstairs. Up on the roof the machine-gunner had finally got his gun in position and started shooting. The truck would almost certainly have been out of range by then.

Of all the positions on this stretch of the front, I was the only one who even noticed the truck as it approached. All the other sentries were sheltering from the rain!

It's perhaps unfair to criticise the YPG too heavily, as plenty of conventional forces suffer from lax discipline and history is replete with cock-ups that resulted in massacres. The YPG is, after all, a militia. But this particular incident wasn't unusual, and the fact that their laziness and incompetence could have got me killed means that I'm happy to be angry about what happened.

As morning had well and truly broken and the whole tabor was awake and actually paying attention, I went into a back room, lit a small fire and lay down to get some sleep. But I was too pumped up, and just lay staring at the ceiling. My fellow sniper came down and asked why I'd not used my Dragunov to engage the truck. I told him that there was enough stupidity about this morning without me adding to it. The range was perfect for AK engagement. It's a more controllable weapon and better for laying down rapid fire. He grinned at that and said that I shouldn't be unhappy: we would be transferring out of this unit soon and that hopefully the day was going to pick up after a miserable start. Unfortunately, it didn't.

We took some bombs from a 120mm mortar later that day, which, in a wrecked shell that's liable to collapse any minute, is not pleasant, and then we heard the news that a foreign volunteer had been killed the day before. Gunter Helsten, a German who'd served in the Foreign Legion and had been with the YPG since Kobane, had been shot in the head during fighting in the centre of town. I'd spoken to him a few days before outside of Shaddadi. 'Don't get killed,' he'd cheerfully said as we'd parted.

On the afternoon of 24 February we got the news that the hospital had been taken and the SDF exalted by firing off automatic volleys into the air. We rejoined the sniper tabor and celebrated. It had been a hard fight in places, and we had taken more casualties than at Al-Hawl, but Daesh had really only committed their usual suicide rear-guard and we had overrun them with a combination of numbers and superior firepower. I admit that this concerned me. The SDF were jubilant and were sure that Daesh were on the road to defeat. That was the case, I was sure, but our enemy was still far from stupid. I had the feeling that if Daesh could devise a way to negate our airpower we would be in real trouble. Shaddadi had shown me that while the SDF troopers were brave, their tactics could be dangerously unimaginative. The quality of the units was also very uneven; some were being extremely competent – thanks to the Darwinian process of combat – but many certainly were not. The successes we were enjoying would disguise fundamental issues in our military system, which would come back to bite us.

However, these concerns couldn't disguise that we had enjoyed a great success and dealt a major blow to ISIS, who were well and truly on the back foot now. I spent that first day as part of the garrison in the hospital and was able to explore the facility at leisure. It was a beautiful building that hadn't even opened before the war had started, and as a result had been slowly gathering dust. Its use by Daesh as a fortress in the last few days meant that it had suffered some damage, mainly where our tanks had shot a few holes in it, but it was still in pretty good condition. I know that the Rojavan parliament had made it a priority to get it back in working order as soon as possible and hope they achieved that, as it had the capability to be the finest medical facility in northern Syria.

Our attentions were soon diverted. Though the town had been taken, Daesh had not gone far, and we spent a few days capturing some of the villages outside the liberated zone so as to expand the defensive perimeter and protect Shaddadi from future attack. This generally went without a hitch; though we had to be careful of ambush or mines and IEDs, we swept through the area in a couple of days. The people were not fleeing us any more: instead, large crowds started to come out to greet us ecstatically, with offerings of tea and food. The civilian population realised that Daesh were gone and that we meant them no harm. No doubt this was handsomely assisted by the copious quantities of cigarettes and tinned food that we distributed, and by how the SDF troops made a huge fuss of every small child that crossed their path. YPG and YPJ troops in particular had a weakness for these tiny bandits, who soon learnt that any passing Kurd would be good for a few sweets.

But we did receive one reminder that the enemy hadn't given up on their claim on the area, and that our new friends were not above hedging their bets. Clearing one large village my team commander – as canny an individual as any – got a feeling about an abandoned and padlocked building. Being an experienced soldier he didn't take the usual SDF approach of kicking the door in (something that plenty of them had learnt to regret, albeit briefly, when they had triggered an IED); he managed to break in and discovered an individual fast asleep – whom he promptly took prisoner. We clustered around the captive with interest while one of the Arab SDF interrogated him. He had the classic Daesh look and regarded us with a combination of fear and hatred. He was tall, at least six and a half feet, and that marked him out as likely not a Syrian, who tend to be short.

'He's not a local,' I said to the team leader. 'Look at the size of him.'

'Yes, he doesn't speak with a local accent either. Maybe a Saudi or a Gulf Arab.'

A crowd of local men had gathered and they began to assure us that they had never seen the man before in their lives, hand to God.

The team leader and I exchanged a look.

'Yeah? So, how did he end up in a house which was locked up from the outside?' I asked him.

'Hah! That is the question, isn't it?' he replied.

One can hardly blame the locals. They had to bend with the wind, and as long as they were not actively working against you there was no problem. Fortunately, the civilians began to accept that the SDF was going to be the new authority in the region and support us and the new government, which under the Rojavan pattern emphasised local authority and autonomy. This is probably the ideal for somewhere with as heterogeneous a population as Syria.

The importance of this support is worth highlighting. Though there would continue to be issues from terrorist attacks throughout northern Syria, these would reduce, and quite often be thwarted, as local intelligence improved and people accepted and began to appreciate the new situation, drying up both local recruits and support for Daesh. People back the side they think is going to win, and the situation here contrasted markedly with what had happened in Afghanistan and Iraq. In both those cases security was reliant upon the firepower of foreign troops, who were inevitably going to leave. Though great efforts were made to train local security forces and establish viable governmental structures, many people retained the belief that these would not survive the inevitable post-occupation power struggle, the result being a resurgent Taliban in Afghanistan and the explosion of ISIS in Iraq.

The difference with the SDF was that they were here to stay. They had defeated the enemy in the field, taken control of the territory and were not leaving, short of being driven out. With no sign of that occurring any time soon the vast majority of people would accept the situation, and go back to their farms and occupations and raise their families.

Following the clearance ops we moved back to Shaddadi

and I started taking every opportunity I could to go wandering around the town looking for anything that might be useful. A major portion of the town – the bit with the nice modern apartment blocks, naturally – had housed significant Daesh forces, and they had abandoned the place in great haste. The streets were littered with military equipment and all sorts of personal items, which was a bonanza for the YPG soldiers, who could re-equip themselves with decent boots and webbing, Daesh equipment as always proving superior to the stuff supplied to us. It also meant there were huge quantities of documents and intelligence literally just blowing in the wind.

Many of the other volunteers had a similar goal in mind and we shared information about areas that we had searched. On my part, a couple of days' digging around produced a bunch of IDs and passports from Indonesia and Russia, and various other bits and pieces. Şêr, the Englishman in sabotage with the bomb-proof head who we had treated back at the mountain camp on our way into Syria, had returned from his quick convalescence in the UK and been especially successful. He'd found a brand new Syrian passport; it was blank, just waiting to be completed with whatever personal details were required. It was apparent that Daesh had the capacity to fake passports for their personnel – a worrying find for sure.

I was sweeping a tower block that had housed Daesh fighters when I made my own discoveries. This was risky, as I was on my own and there were no lights, meaning that I was taking real care to minimise my noise and cover everything with my weapon. I couldn't be sure that all booby traps had been cleared, though for the most part all the buildings had been pillaged by SDF fighters or the few remaining civilians around.

What caught my attention was that the door of one flat had a warning on it. In English. It warned that the curses of Allah would fall upon any who intruded, and various other dire threats concerning those who did the devil's work. And it concluded that the owner had official documents proving his right to residence and he would seek legal recompense against anyone who damaged his property. So there.

I must admit the contrast brought a chuckle from me. The notice had also had zero effect on the SDF guys who'd preceded me, and they'd ransacked the place with gusto. But they and I were looking for different things. The flat was beautifully decorated with inscriptions carefully painted on the wall, all quotations from the Quran. In French.

'Bingo,' I said to myself.

I checked through the detritus all over the floor before carefully checking the cupboards and drawers. I'm no IED expert, but I know to be slow and cautious before touching anything that might conceal a trip switch or wire; I'd heard too many horror stories about what happened to the careless.

My search turned up a few bits of ID and some other documents, but, best of all, was a notebook kept by a Brit who'd joined ISIS. In it was the start of a diary, some basic words and sentences in Arabic, and a mass of contact details, phone numbers and email addresses.

Jackpot. This was exactly the sort of information that the British authorities would want to get their hands on.

The diary I turned over to YPG intelligence – I wasn't willing to risk their wrath if I got caught holding out on them. But there was nothing to stop me taking hi-res photos of everything I thought of interest and sending them to the Special Branch police who had come to see me before I'd returned to Syria. To my mind, supplying the authorities with useful information could only boost the war effort against Daesh. Of course, the Kurds had a very different take on this ideal, which was demonstrated to me all too clearly a few days later.

I had just come back from one of my scrounging missions – with no success – when I walked into my billet to be confronted by a very suspicious-looking character, who seemed to be nosing around. The well-made uniform, bushy beard and top-of-the-range dark glasses marked him out as one of the Special Forces soldiers. The fact he wasn't wearing a baseball cap and looked smart made me suspect he wasn't one of the Americans I'd encountered on the day we'd been attacked by the suicide car.

'*Bonjour, mon ami. Ça va?*' I hazarded.

I was correct. He promptly rattled off a stream of French that was, I'm afraid, completely beyond me. Fortunately, I am capable of saying 'Sorry, I don't understand' in more than a dozen languages. He then signalled me to follow him outside where, waiting for me, must have been a substantial part of the French effort in Syria at that time. Their boss spoke passable English, and between that and my pidgin French he was able to tell me they'd heard about the British sniper who was prowling around looking for intel and asked if I could give them any pointers about where they might conduct their own searches.

I was delighted to help them, and immediately told them

about the flat with French writing on the walls. They were suitably enthusiastic about the prospect of finding something useful.

So absorbed were we in our conversation that I didn't notice that a small Kurd had sidled up until he poked me in the arm. I looked at him and said:

'Yes, friend?'

'Hello,' he replied.

I waited for a few seconds but nothing else seemed to be forthcoming, so I resumed my conversation with the French commander. Until I felt another nudge on my arm. This time it was one of the snipers from my unit. He was nervously shuffling from foot to foot.

'We need to talk,' he said. Eyeing the French soldiers, he added:

'In private.'

Making my excuses, we moved away so he could tell me what was so important.

'What's up?' I asked.

'You have to stop talking to them. He's not happy,' he said, nodding his head over to the Kurd who'd first come up to me and was now, I noticed, glaring daggers at me.

'Why?'

'They're soldiers. He's in charge of them. He doesn't want them looking around.'

I considered this for a few seconds.

'Tell him I talk to who I like.'

And then I went back to the French lads, who confirmed that they had been requesting permission to search through the ruins but had been fobbed off or only allowed into areas that had been sterilised of intelligence. Hence their reason for seeking me out.

To be fair, the treatment of the Kurds by foreign powers means they have developed an inevitable suspicion of outside parties claiming to be friends. But when it came to this issue, I held the view, and still do, that sharing intelligence can only be of benefit in fighting Daesh, not just in Syria and Iraq, but around the world.

The French weren't the only ones looking for my assistance. The next day a Norwegian YPG volunteer came to ask my advice. He'd found something that he wanted my opinion on.

Sure, no worries.

He produced a small glass vial of clear liquid from his pocket and said:

'I found this with a load of old gas masks. Do you know anything about chemical weapons?'

You know those times, we've all had them I'm sure, when a voice in your head stands up and screams, but you really don't want to show how utterly terrified you are in case it makes the situation much, much worse.

I have something of a layman's knowledge of chemical weapons from university and from my previous studies of the subject and, after hearing that Daesh had used things like mustard gas in Iraq recently, I had bolstered this knowledge by emailing military friends for advice on how to deal with the threat, particularly treatment of casualties.

And now here I was, face to face with what could possibly be a nerve agent, which the Assad regime was known to have stockpiled and used earlier in the conflict. It was not a pleasant feeling.

'You need to show me where you found this. Right now. Is there any more?'

I glanced at the innocent-looking vial in his hand.

'And you need to be fucking careful with that.'

He led me to a smashed-up office building. Inside it was littered with old Syrian uniforms and ancient gas masks that looked like they had been there for years, so covered with dust were they. And there were a number of little boxes that contained more of the glass vials, with French instructions written on the inside of the box lids.

I began to breathe easier. The vials appeared, from what I could tell, to be testing kits *for* chemical weapons. There were warnings in the instructions that the kits themselves were toxic, but I could relax as one mistake wouldn't kill everything several hundred metres downwind from us.

Though this event ended OK, there were other discoveries that were a reminder of why we were there. We found a number of what were described as 'rape houses'. These places were where women enslaved by Daesh were kept for communal use. Many of them were Yazidis who had been captured at the massacre at the Shingal mountain, and one major impetus for our breakneck drive had been to free these women, especially as our intelligence reported that Daesh planned to murder them to prevent their liberation. Unfortunately, Daesh had managed to remove the women before we could encircle the town, and all that was left to see were the remains of their treatment.

The house didn't look like much from outside, but inside the floor was covered in a mass of soiled mattresses. Huge quantities of condoms, spermicide, lubricants and antibiotics were strewn all over the place. Carefully picking through the debris in the hope of finding some evidence of the identities of the women who'd been held, I felt a palpable sense of evil in the air, like we were being contaminated by being in this place. Perhaps it was the knowledge of what had happened here, the suffering and the misery, that was influencing my imagination, but it felt like a dark presence lurked and I began to feel a great and mounting rage deep inside. I wasn't the only one to be affected. My team commander, generally a very calm and measured man, spat on the floor as we left.

'*Daesh pîs*,' he snarled, a term indicating something is evil in a completely literal sense.

One of the younger snipers held up an unused condom.

'What is it?' he asked.

The team commander snapped at him to drop it and then, looking very worn, said to me, 'Sometimes I forget how young many of the hevals are.' He himself was only in his late twenties, but the old hands had all been aged by the war. They'd seen too many friends and colleagues die along the way. Few YPG soldiers made it to thirty.

In many abandoned houses we found nooses hanging from the rafters. This caused some confusion, as suicide is *haram* under Islamic law, a great sin. And then it was explained to us that these houses had belonged to Daesh fighters and their families who'd purchased slave girls. In the event that the SDF advance had trapped them before they could escape, the nooses were ready to string up the unfortunate slaves so that we could not save them.

The foreign volunteers were both horrified and enraged by these discoveries and this was noted by our Kurdish and Arab colleagues. An order came down that under no circumstance were Daesh prisoners to be left with foreign volunteers. I'm not saying that anything would have happened, but it was probably a wise move by the generals.

Daesh might have been defeated in Shaddadi, but they were far from finished. A major force attacked from Turkey, overrunning the border guards and reaching as far as the city of Saluk. If they had succeeded they would have cut Rojava in two and things could have been very difficult for us. Fortunately Saluk, which had been largely abandoned in the previous year, was strongly garrisoned as it was to be the springboard for a new assault set to launch imminently. In a night of heavy fighting the Daesh force was shredded by the SDF and comprehensively wiped out, though not before they had killed at least one hundred civilians, from what I was told.

With hindsight this offensive was to prove to be Daesh's 'Battle of the Bulge'; a last throw of the dice with whatever resources had been carefully marshalled to launch such a surprise offensive to try to break the momentum that the SDF had built up. But at the time we could only hear the distant news and wonder what other surprises might await us.

We also faced some local counterattacks around Shaddadi, and on the night of 28 February Daesh managed to seize back one of the villages recently liberated on the outskirts of the town. This attack went as well as the counter-offensive in the north, and was crushed, quite literally, after an SDF BMP armoured vehicle smashed through a house and squashed the four Daesh who were sheltering there. Their comrades took the point and ran for it.

The 1st of March saw us on the march again. The YPG had spent months fighting a gruelling war in the Abdul Aziz mountains. As they form a natural defensive and observation line across the battle zone they had been savagely fought over by the YPG and Daesh, and now the SDF stood on the high ground, having succeeded in driving the enemy off the peaks. The front had stabilised, with Daesh dug in down on the plains at the foot of the range.

From Shaddadi we would sweep west, well away from the mountains and Daesh's front line. Meanwhile the Saluk battle group would push south and east to meet us. If we were quick enough we could cut off Daesh, as well as liberating hundreds of villages and some ten thousand square kilometres of territory.

Progress was good in that first morning, and we advanced through several villages so quickly that the bemused residents didn't even attempt to flee. They just watched with confused smiles as a vast convoy of Hiluxes, smothered in beaming and waving fighters of both sexes, passed their homes and pressed on. Unfortunately, in the afternoon we took mortar fire, indicating that Daesh had figured out what we were doing and were setting up defences. From now we would have to treat each hamlet as potentially hostile and approach with caution.

One of the ways that high command hoped to catch more Daesh in the net was to advance through the night. We set out in a vast convoy running with no lights so as to try to disguise our progress. The issue with this for our unit was that very few of the YPG were qualified to drive and also, due to the terrible rate of crashes (no doubt a consequence of giving young adults who routinely faced death access to a brand-new vehicle and long, straight roads which allowed one to get up a good head of steam), there was a standard punishment of an immediate ban for any soldiers who suffered an accident. Consequently our drivers were loath to risk their licences on such trips, and I found myself in the driver's seat for this advance. It was nerve-racking as we would only be able to see anything if a vehicle in front applied its brakes. Quite often we drove utterly blind, craning to see through the windscreen and straining eyes against the darkness as we crawled forward. As if this wasn't bad enough, we were constantly aware that if we ran across a Daesh IED or ambush we'd be sitting ducks. Fortunately on the night of 4 March the horizon was awash with the lights from vehicles that signified the advance of the Saluk battlegroup. They were heading towards us and we were able to link up with them the following day and close our cordon. We had created a pocket with a vast tract of Daesh territory inside needing to be cleared. We also had to watch the outer edge of the pocket as Daesh would no doubt try to attack us if they detected any weakness.

Ironically, my main concern as regards the welfare of my fellows wasn't Daesh, though they did insist on firing anti-tank guided missiles at us from time to time, but the cold and wet weather. The sort of mobile warfare we were engaged in meant we often had to sleep in our vehicles or outside. Most of the fighters developed hacking coughs and every day saw a miserable line of sufferers queuing at the ambulance accompanying us, where the medics dished out antibiotics like sweets.

We'd taken a comparatively large village and this became our headquarters while the new perimeter was shored up.

Here we retained substantial forces to act as a quick reaction force in the event of a major Daesh attack on the line. Meanwhile, small bases, ranging from holding a fire team to a tabor, were built every couple of kilometres to form the new front. These were very basic affairs, little more than a circular berm thrown up by a digger to stop suicide cars. Some of the larger ones housed dushkas, but generally any unit based there was reliant on whatever weapons they had to hand.

For the snipers, our job was to provide night sentries. This entailed us scanning the horizon with our thermal scopes, watching for any sign of attack. The plain around us appeared flat and featureless, but actually hid many nooks and wadis, some of which ran straight into Daesh territory and allowed the potential for an assault force to pop up anywhere.

Of course, the hard-baked plain may have seemed as lifeless as it was featureless, but again this was deceptive. At night the place would come alive with animals bustling all over the place. Though our scopes were very good they were just commercially available hunting models and as such any sudden hot spot had to be carefully scrutinised. This led to me terrifying one YPG soldier who came over to see if everything was all clear. I was scanning the terrain when he wandered over to ask if he could have a look, a standard request from bored sentries who loved how our sights could pierce the pitch darkness.

'Anything happening?' he asked.

'No, nothing out there at the—'

A glowing head had just appeared about three hundred metres away, from a wadi that ran straight into Daesh land.

'Botan?' the soldier asked.

In Kachin State, Burma, inspecting the front line between the Kachin Independence Army and the Tatmadaw (Burmese Army)

An American and an Arakan FBR trainer. The motto is the same, one in Shan and the other in English

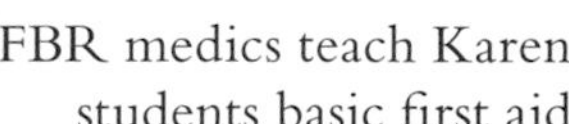

FBR medics teach Karen students basic first aid

Taking my three shots on the PKM machine gun

A turret from a Daesh T72 tank in Kobane. The YPG salvaged and reused anything they could in this early stage of the war

Three foreign volunteers return from a shopping trip in Kobane. Water, coffee and baklava – part of why we loved the city so much, along with the affection the residents showed us

Taking a break out of the heat, Kobane

The school where Daesh infiltrators murdered more than one hundred children and their teachers in June 2015

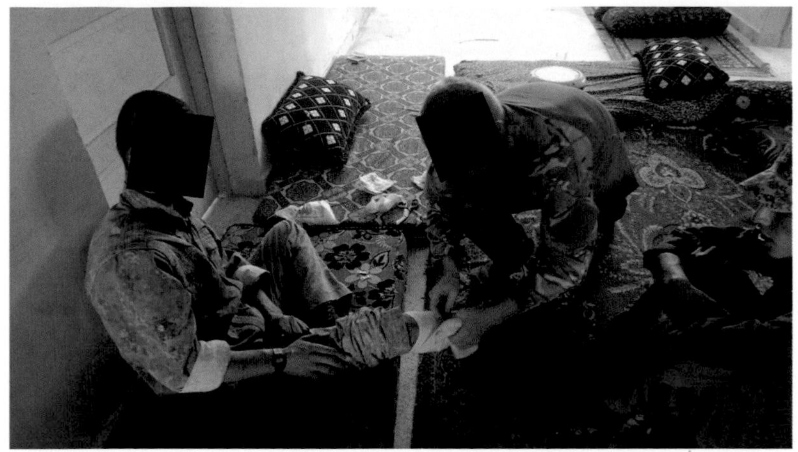

Soro, the English medic, treats an injured YPG fighter, Sarrin

Our position guarding the inlet on the Euphrates. Daesh's one attempt at crossing met short shrift from machine guns mounted on the overlooking slopes

Del Gesh forming the first YPG cavalry unit

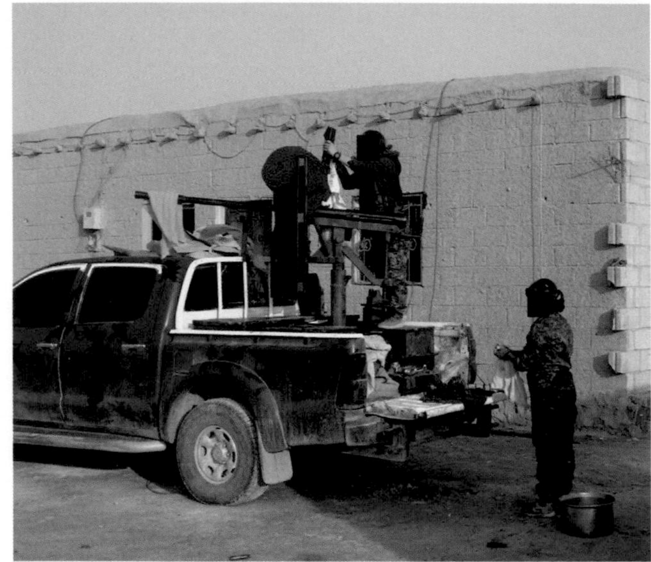

A YPJ crew clean their dushka. After airstrikes, these were the primary form of fire support for the SDF

My squad commander engaging Daesh fighters with a Zagros heavy rifle

Playing sardines in an MTLB while charging in to the attack. A terrifying experience

Shelter in the frontline set-ups was extremely basic, but welcome after days of nothing but the ground

A YPG T55. Though impressive to see in action, I was quite sceptical of their efficacy after witnessing them generally miss whatever it was they were aiming at

The sniper team taking it easy after the fall of Shadaddi

The snipers' rooftop position when guarding the front. Here, it is still under construction, but would soon boast multiple fire points, segregating blast walls and storage for observation devices

Watching from our observation point. The blankets were strung so as to maximise the cover they gave from the sun during the hottest parts of the day, while not obscuring the view of the surrounding terrain

My weapons. The white tape on the Dragunov's magazine indicated that it was loaded with armour-piercing incendiary bullets for use against VBIEDs – somewhat forlorn, as most by this point were too heavily armoured for the Dragunov to penetrate, but still better than standard anti-personnel rounds

An MTLB of the Manbij Military Council, part of the SDF, flies its flag high

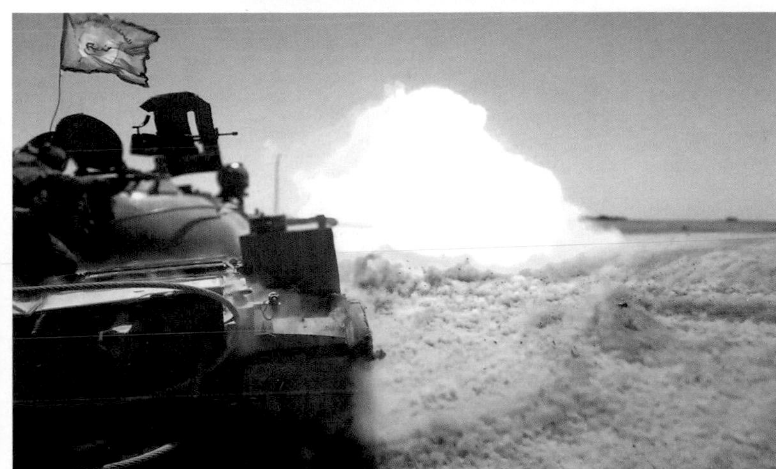

A YPG tank in action on the drive towards Manbij

Coalition airstrike

View of Manbij from one of our loopholes. Observation of the terrain, especially for subtle changes, was key to dealing with Daesh

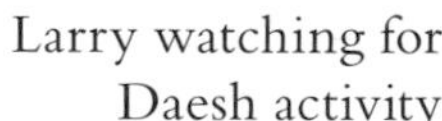

Larry watching for Daesh activity

Resting in the olive grove between shots. The grove was an excellent place to shoot from as it offered plenty of cover, multiple places to fire from and was in sight of a large section of the front we responsible for

Heval Bermal, one of the YPJ snipers, demonstrating the love of children that all YPJ and YPG seemed to share. Bermal, one of the sniper tabor's squad commanders, was killed in the fighting for Tabqa dam in early 2017

I didn't reply. The head was staring straight at us. I flicked the safety off the M16 and settled the aiming point dead centre. The moment whoever it was showed a weapon or the slightest hint of aggression I was going to shoot them in the centre of their face.

'*Botan?*' the soldier whimpered. He realised that things might be about to go bad and there was a total of six of us to hold what was little more than a scrape in the ground, with no support particularly close.

'Shhh . . . ' I hissed, letting my breath out so as to both tell him to be quiet and slow my heartbeat for the shot.

The head continued to stare at us. The aiming point was dead still in the centre of the target. I squeezed the trigger, letting the pressure build up to the breaking point that would fire the weapon . . .

The head turned, and I was now looking at the profile of a dog. I took a long breath, put the safety back on and lowered the rifle.

'Just a dog,' I told my companion, who sighed deeply in relief.

The thermal scopes may have been a boon for watching, but their use had its risks, especially if you were stupid enough to walk around while using them. Like me.

I was on guard at the main village. To get as good a view as possible we set up a position on top of an abandoned house, which gave us an uninterrupted 360-degree view. Being woken every night at random times can make one somewhat dozy, especially when what sleep you do get tends to be in the cold and on the wet ground. So I was not on best form, even before standing in the wind hoisting a rifle for two hours.

Sweeping as usual I caught sight of something warm moving. It was likely another one of the dogs that seem to wander the whole of northern Syria in the night, like the one that had nearly got shot previously, but I needed to make sure that the heat signature, which was some distance away, wasn't a threat. With the scope clamped to my eye I took a few steps forward, trying to get a better view. I could see the rooftop in front of me, at the bottom of the scope's view screen. Unfortunately I had forgotten that this building had a stepped roof with a brick lip on the edge, and the contrast in the thermal scope did not show that. The result was me clipping my foot and pitching head-first onto the lower roof with an almighty crash and a scream.

I lay stunned and in considerable pain for a minute before I had to drag myself up. I hadn't, after all, confirmed that the object that had caused my misfortune was not a Daesh infiltrator, and as no other sentry seemed to have heard a sudden scream in the night, or if they did hadn't bothered to investigate, I had better make sure that we were not about to be attacked.

My first thought was panic that I had broken the scope. No, it was fine, and the mystery object was indeed another dog. My second thought was that the rifle had been damaged when I had landed on it. A fumbled check in the dark revealed that it too seemed fine. My third thought was that I might have cracked my skull, which was agonising. I gingerly felt my head. I could feel blood pouring down my face, soaking my uniform so that it clung to my chest. I'd taken a heck of a blow but, unable to use a mirror or a light, it wasn't possible to tell just how bad. My neck also started to ache abominably from the strain it had suffered.

I only had a short period of guard duty left and so was able to wake up my relief and then slump down into my blankets, where I passed out. The fun started the next morning when I walked out for breakfast looking like I'd been the victim of an axe attack, to the horror of the rest of my tabor. Once they realised I wasn't likely to die, having failed to expire in the night, their concerns soon turned to mockery which was, admittedly, entirely deserved.

Dying through my own idiocy was not, however, the only threat. Daesh may have been caught out by our lightning advance but were still intent on being difficult, and it was here that my deep hatred of drones, or at least the Daesh ones, was to begin. The choking dust our advances had thrown up, and the hard beatings of driving across country, obviously meant our vehicles had a tough time of it, so a mobile mechanic tabor came out to the new front HQ and started servicing any vehicles that could be spared. Oil and fluids were checked and refreshed, brakes and chassis examined, and an air compressor used to blow clean the clogged air filters.

While this was going on I took the opportunity to chew the fat with the commander of 223, the tabor made up of foreign veterans. The SDF may have been dismissive of such ideas, but there was no denying that they appreciated the effectiveness of the unit. As we stood and talked over the situation and what the outside world was doing to help, we became aware of a buzzing noise overhead. Looking around we caught sight of a small aircraft slowly drifting along above us. It was your classic short-range reconnaissance drone, a glorified model aircraft but no doubt fitted with a live-streaming video camera.

'Any of the Special Forces guys got one of those?' I enquired. I knew that the French used quadcopters, but had never seen this sort of UAV in use before.

'Reckon that's Daesh,' said the commander of 223.

And with that the mortar bombs started falling on us. The cluster of vehicles and personnel was obviously just the sort of target our interloper had been searching for and he started directing fire onto us. There followed a panicked scramble as drivers leapt into their vehicles and shot away, and the mechanics threw their tools into their trucks and departed with just as much haste. We were lucky that, though the drone had picked us out, the Daesh mortar crew was not so good and scattered projectiles all over the base area. I lay in a scrape by the outer berm and stared up at the departing machine. This was the start of a deep antagonism I felt for these things, which I have difficulty explaining. Perhaps it was the feeling of being like a mouse with a hawk overhead, or having someone obviously watching you while intending you harm. I don't know. I do know that from then on I would have a pathological hatred for drones and whenever I heard their whining tone overhead I would seize my rifle and charge onto any rooftop, scanning the skies and looking to kill them.

ISIS mortars and Katyusha rockets were the biggest irritation, and though we faced only a few concerted barrages, as when the drone came over, it wasn't unusual to receive several pieces of ordnance randomly most days. My ability to judge the fall of these had become quite acute and I rarely even worried about them, as I could predict their fall quite accurately from the sound of the projectiles' travel through the air. However, during one tac mil we were lucky that the house we snipers had been allocated was a well-built concrete building that had been further fortified with earth heaped up against its outside walls for blast absorption. While we sat in discussion on the veranda a rocket came down with a screaming *whoosh* just on the other side of the house, less than ten metres away. The house and its impromptu additions did their job and saved us from being obliterated, though we were all left with ringing ears. Of course, the slightest variation in the rocket's trajectory would have killed or wounded the entire sniper team. But such are the vagaries and random factors of war, and if you are going to worry about how much luck and/or fate play in your survival you are in the wrong place.

On 7 March we advanced against the main Daesh position left inside the pocket, a small town and an old Syrian military base. After a day of fighting we were able to clear them out and that was pretty much the end of the operation. Daesh made one last desperate attempt to attack us with a huge VBIED. This was a large truck, heavily armoured and carrying at least ten tonnes of explosives, judging from the blast. From about two kilometres away I watched as it raced towards its target. And then I watched as a nearby Javelin crew calmly locked on and fired. The missile hissed into the air and less than half a minute later the charging truck exploded in a titanic conflagration, with a mushroom cloud that reminded me more of a nuclear blast than anything conventional. The bomb, and its driver, had achieved nothing.

The new front had been established, and new infantry units from local brigades and the Asayish paramilitary police moved in to garrison the positions we had dug out on the line of our advance. A team from the sniper tabor stayed behind to back up these procedures, but the rest of us packed up our gear and headed back to base at Sari Kani, looking forward to a chance to wash ourselves and our clothes properly.

The liberation of Shaddadi and the subsequent rapid operation to keep pressure on Daesh had been a great success, and the SDF had demonstrated its much improved operational planning and execution capability. There was still scope for improvement and I had concerns about what would happen if we hit serious resistance, but the fact was that the SDF was starting to show a real ability to be the country's most effective fighting force against Daesh, especially from the point of view of the Americans and their coalition allies.

The SDF spearhead had charged headlong through enemy villages, or bypassed them altogether, leaving follow-up forces to deal with any resistance and, though we hadn't managed to capture major enemy forces in the encirclements, the signs of a hurried departure and the amount of equipment strewn about in Shaddadi showed it had been a close-run thing. As I understood it we had captured more than ten thousand square kilometres of territory and hundreds of towns and villages. We also cut a major road that linked Daesh territories in Iraq and Syria.

The SDF reported that we had lost twenty-six killed and thirteen injured in the battle for Shaddadi, while Daesh lost 455 killed. I don't know how accurate this is as I was to later learn that the official releases, especially as regards casualties, were often fudged, with the names of the dead being released over time to make it appear that deaths occurred at later dates and lessen the impression of serious casualties.

*

The evolving attitude of civilians in this campaign was noticeable. For the first time they began to view the SDF not as some awful threat but instead as a group that they could coexist with, and which was also on the rise. The writing was on the wall for Daesh and the SDF was, at least for the foreseeable future, going to be the de facto controller of the region.

There was, alas, one major hitch. During the suicide attack on the outskirts of Shaddadi, someone had filmed the engagement. As we finished the campaign this footage had found its way to the international press, who had managed to break it down until they had a still of the moment just before destruction. There, plain as day, could be seen a Javelin on its final dive onto the target.

The Turks, needless to say, went utterly insane. If I had been surprised to find this weapon suddenly in our inventory, they were apoplectic. While we fought a massive international row erupted and, at the end of the campaign, our Javelins were withdrawn.

9

Guarding the Front and Meeting New Friends

March–May 2016

Back in our base in Sari Kani, the rest of the sniper tabor set about going through the post-operational processes of cleaning and storing weapons and equipment, and conducting tac mils to assess performance and address grievances. They also immediately undertook further ideological training. While I was willing to contribute to my squad and tabor tac mils, my presence at the bigger debriefs was largely pointless as my Kurdish really wasn't up to following the proceedings. The fact that such affairs could drag on for days, and even weeks, meant that I was happy to forego the pleasure and stay at the barracks as guard. I was soon joined by some welcome company.

First to roll in was Hozan, a Canadian volunteer who had fought at Shaddadi in an infantry tabor and wanted to try the snipers out. As we had the days to ourselves we developed a basic exercise to work on our camouflage techniques. Although many think of Syria as a desert, Rojava is actually the bread basket of the country. In the spring the wheat grows thick and lush, and has a truly remarkable colour, literally an emerald green that glistens and shines brilliantly in the sunshine. A field of this crop sat behind our base and we used it to practise in. We would take it in turns, one of us having to find a position where we could line up our rifle (with no ammunition, I hasten to add) as though for a shot, while the other took position on our roof and gave the shooter two minutes to position themselves before starting a search through a powerful pair of binoculars. The shooter couldn't duck away; he had to maintain his shooting position and scope view of the target – the other player. It certainly passed the time and was a very useful exercise, allowing us both to experiment with our techniques and camouflage. This may sound obvious, but things like camouflaging a weapon are critical. Get it wrong and an enemy will spot your rifle, with obvious results. Of particular interest to me was how my new British Multi-Terrain Pattern (MTP) camouflage performed. Though it was generally excellent, Hozan reported that when I attempted to leopard crawl down the hill the pattern actually shone in the bright sunlight and caught his eye.

We were soon joined by a couple of other foreigners, one of them a Swedish soldier I will call Larry, who I would go on to see some serious combat alongside. I didn't have time for more than a cursory introduction to these two as I did not stay at Sari Kani for very long. As the political situation seemed to preclude any further advances against ISIS while the Turks went spare at our successes, on 15 March I volunteered to go back to the front to replace the team we had left to support the new front line. A new squad was assembled, and we headed back out to where we had been less than a week before. It was much changed. A suicide vehicle had managed to get past the berm and had detonated inside the village. Incredibly, there had only been a few light casualties. The outer berm had subsequently been extensively built up, with false entrances to confuse any more VBIEDs. The actual entrance was now a complex, winding affair that was difficult to negotiate even when you knew where you were going!

Additionally, berms had been built around all of the buildings, earth had been piled onto the roofs as impromptu cover for firing from, and bunkers had been constructed on the ground for taking refuge from mortars and rockets. These came several times a day and would actually be welcome distractions on most days, as there was little to do. In fact, the month or so we spent at the front was one of those situations where the hours would drag on and on . . . then something would happen that would make things suddenly interesting.

Generally, that meant getting rocketed. Several times a day you could expect a rocket to explode somewhere in the area. Fortunately, their inherent inaccuracy meant that these were normally kilometres away from anything important, and they would detonate harmlessly on the plain. But sometimes one would crash into a compound, spraying shrapnel all over the place.

With plenty of time on our hands, and the ever-present threat of attack, our little sniper squad set about improving our fortifications. The first thing we did was sandbag the top of the earth parapet on our roof. If you lay on heaped earth to shoot you had very little protection from return fire. By sandbagging and creating dedicated interlocking fire positions any attack would be met with withering fire from our position while we stayed in relative safety. Once again, the wreckage of the suicide bomb provided a useful haul. The armour plate, which was blown all over the village in twisted segments, was gathered up and used to strengthen our loopholes further.

Hozan and I then set about improving our squad's watch position. This far south the heat and sun were fierce, so we dug out a large iron bed frame with a sheet metal base and mounted it on the sandbagged wall. With a few spare blankets strung up between the legs, this gave both cover from the sun and from observation by the enemy, while allowing us to keep watch. We even rigged a ladder so that a person could climb up onto the top of this rather Heath Robinson affair and see for a considerable distance in all directions.

When the heat of the day got too much, Hozan and I would spend hours sitting up in our shelter watching the Daesh lines through powerful binoculars. It was five or six kilometres to the villages that the enemy held, but we kept a log of vehicle movements. We also identified the points where Daesh seemed to have stashed their rockets and launching rails. There were several of these and the Daesh crews made a point of using different ones each time, but by watching we soon were able to identify the key points that the rockets generally came from, and also spot the signs that one was being set up for an attack and issue warnings.

Most of the other positions forming the front were garrisoned by either Asayish or local defence tabors. Both tended to be inexperienced and jittery, and this meant many of our nights were interrupted by sudden bursts of fire as an overexcited sentry got spooked. I was used to this from the campaigns I had fought in, and as a result was quite capable of sleeping through them. Hozan once marvelled how he had kicked me awake during one of these false alerts, just for me to open my eyes, listen for five seconds before mumbling 'Asayish', and then immediately start to snore again. This may seem like laziness, but if I suddenly sprang up and darted to a fire position he understood that there really was a serious problem. We were all pulling several hours a night doing watches with our thermal scopes, and getting up before dawn as that was the favoured time for Daesh to attack, so nothing short of a full assault would get me out of my blankets.

While back at the village I made the acquaintance of a couple of volunteers who would go on to be close friends and comrades. Moe and Curly had come out to the SDF to help found the Tactical Medical Unit, a dedicated medical tabor largely composed of foreign veterans, which had been set up when the critical shortage of competent medical personnel had been recognised by some volunteers. They had since left the unit and, at a loose end and looking for a new tabor, had gravitated to the front and been placed with one of the garrison units. Both had extensive military backgrounds, were very fit and stood out even among the other former soldiers as extremely competent. They, like us, had set about improving the defences of their unit and built a rather excellent fire point in the front wall of the berm which faced Daesh.

This was the general pattern: we'd work on our bunker,

chat with Curly and Moe when they came round, and watch Daesh, who would shoot occasional rockets at our positions, and the Asayish would have panic attacks in the night time. The weeks drifted along.

It all changed when, surprise, surprise, the drone turned up. And people wonder why I hate them.

It was 29 April and I was washing up after dinner – our usual fare of spaghetti with a spoonful of tomato paste stirred into it – using an outdoor water tank and standing in the sunshine when I heard a faint buzz. For a second I thought it was a mosquito, surprising in this dry landscape, but then realised my mistake and snapped my eyes to the sky. There, hanging like a bird of prey, was the unmistakable shape of the mini-aircraft directly overhead. And I didn't have a weapon to hand.

The drone went on its way and, despite its progress being reported on the radio and some of the positions putting up fire to try to down it, surveyed a large section of our front as it went. No doubt Daesh got a good deal of information about our dispositions. They certainly started getting more lively and accurate with their rockets, which began to routinely target our village and the neighbouring positions with greater intensity. They had also identified where our dushkas and armoured personnel carriers were kept, as this location started taking a lot of narrow misses, and there was even a direct hit on the corner of the large building that the crews lived in. Fortunately the only casualty was a sentry, who suffered some minor shrapnel wounds.

We had another surprise from our riled-up neighbours. The Daesh positions were all between four and six kilometres away, except for one solitary house that stood on its own three kilometres from us. Hozan and I had kept an eye on it because its position made it an excellent possible forward observation post for Daesh. Sure enough, one day it suddenly sprouted a heavy machine gun on a tripod, which proceeded to open fire at us from extreme range.

I must admit that, by not taking the threat as seriously as I should, I nearly met my end. The position in front of us was taking the brunt of the fire, but it was apparent that the rounds were not hitting the building directly but bouncing on the ground in front of our berm before ricocheting up and hitting the house. Knowing this, and located further back, I stood behind my sandbags and watched the Daesh machine-gunners servicing their weapons. We were waiting to see if one of our dushkas could be brought up to engage them, or else an airstrike summoned. As such, and thinking I was out of range of the gun, I wanted to watch what they did so that I could communicate where they went to the gunners or aircraft if they tried to hide away from return fire. My standing there with a pair of binoculars was evidently noted by the Daesh crew's own observer.

'Get down, dumbass,' shouted Hozan from behind me, where he had sensibly ducked down behind one of the thick walls we had built to minimise the risk from rocket shrapnel landing on the roof.

'Nah. It's OK. They can't hit us from here,' I assured him.

THWACK

A round smacked solidly into a sandbag ten feet from me. Considering the range, and that they were bouncing the bullets off the hard-baked ground, it was a pretty impressive shot. It was certainly enough to make me dive behind the barricade (and appreciate all the hours and sweat we had put into it) as more pounded into the packed bags.

Needless to say, if they could hit us, we could hit them, and our team leader came onto the roof with his Zagros. Taking careful aim, with me spotting for him, he had to estimate the range as best he could as he had dialled his sight out to its maximum and needed to adjust his fire to hit. The rifle looked more like a cannon as he pointed it up in the air to get the bullet out to that range. The first three rounds fell short, but with my direction he was able to hit the house with his fourth. This was enough to convince the Daesh machine-gunners that sticking around was a bad idea, and they hurried to drag their weapon under cover.

'Do you want a go?' the team leader asked me and Hozan. 'Put the house at the bottom of the reticule and you can hit it.'

Having had a narrow squeak, I was more than happy to return the favour. It was also tremendously satisfying to gradually demolish a building at three kilometres with a rifle. Most of the rounds landed around the hut, but those that hit blew lumps out of the roof and dropped pieces into the interior. It's unlikely that we hit anyone, but Daesh took the hint.

The attention we were receiving from Daesh couldn't be allowed to continue without response. First, a YPG mortar crew turned up. To reach the closest Daesh positions required a 120mm mortar, a substantial weapon that requires a lot of training and experience to use. Here we were to have an advantage, in that for a change we had some capable operators on hand.

After the crew fired off a handful of rounds, most of which disappeared into the tree line of the Daesh villages and thus left us guessing as to their actual impact, Moe and Curly asked if they could each have a bomb to fire. As both had received training on these sorts of weapons they were able to set them correctly, landing their bombs directly in a compound that we had seen a truck using several times a day and was thought to be a Daesh logistics post.

However, this was to be just the first attempt to inflict some harm on our awkward neighbours. It was decided that the snipers would send out a patrol to try to find out what was going on over there and, if possible, cull a few Daesh in the night. The team was made up of two snipers, my team leader and me, all carrying M16s with thermal scopes. We would be supported by a two-man machine gun team with a PKM.

Our target was four kilometres away and had been flagged as a possible rocket crew hideout, but we would dogleg our route to avoid a direct approach and known enemy strongpoints. The walk across no man's land was over open terrain with hidden wadis that, on a moonless night, made the passage both treacherous and exposed. We two snipers led, periodically checking through our scopes for enemy activity. The plan was to approach the target house, place the machine gun at four hundred metres and then observe with the thermals. If any Daesh were seen we would sneak forward as close as possible, engage as many targets as was practical and then retreat while the machine gun covered us. The mission had considerable risks. Though I was confident in both my team leader and my own abilities, the machine gun crew would not be able to see anything in the pitch black and we would have to worry about getting hit by their fire as well as any from Daesh forces. Though we talked through how the mission should play out, there were a lot of unknowns and a night operation like this could get complicated very quickly. We also had the issue that if anyone was wounded the likelihood of being able to evacuate them across several miles of open ground with an alert enemy was negligible. The mission was scheduled for the night of 1 May.

We stripped down to carry just weapons and ammunition, and departed at 9 p.m. We scrambled over the perimeter berm and, being careful to avoid where we knew SDF mines had been laid, struck out into the gloom. We had certainly chosen the right night. The darkness was impenetrable and we walked slowly so as to minimise our noise and avoid falling on the many obstacles. Wadis, small irrigation ditches and rutted fields criss-crossed the plain, and though they might not seem much in the daylight, in the dark they resulted in constant stumbles. Going too fast would pitch you on your face, with all the sound that entailed.

We stopped every two hundred metres to scan the terrain, the team leader checking the route ahead while I would look to the flanks for any sign of activity. We progressed at a snail's pace until we suddenly received some unexpected help. A low grumble approached and the team leader's radio, set as low as he could have it and still hear anything, started to crackle. Our mission had been checked in to the central command post at Euphrates Volcano to ensure we didn't get attacked by mistake by coalition aircraft, and the Americans, with resources to spare, had dispatched an AC-130 gunship and a jet of some description to watch over us. We received orders to hunker down so that the circling gunship could acquire our location and communicate back that they had us.

It was slightly disconcerting to be sitting waiting for the gunship to make its identification; being circled by an aircraft that can hit you with a range of heavy ordnance right out of the blue is a bit worrying, and we had to hope the crew weren't trigger happy and had got accurate information about us. But we soon got the all clear and were able to proceed. The aircraft were something of a mixed blessing. With the thermal sights they could see everything moving around us for miles, which meant that we didn't have to worry so much about being ambushed. But this was balanced by the fact that the persistent presence of the aircraft would let Daesh know that something was afoot, and they would keep their heads down.

In spite of the presence of our mother hens we approached the Daesh zone of control carefully. The whole area was pitted with Daesh earthworks and trenches and we bypassed them with extreme caution, watching them carefully through our scopes. Nothing stirred. We settled down to watch the target house, which sat right in the middle of what appeared to be a heavily defended area.

An hour passed. Despite our constant surveillance of both the target and the surrounding terrain, we had seen nothing at all: no guards, no civilians, no domestic animals, not even a dog. It was unnaturally quiet.

'What do you think?' I asked my team leader.

He said nothing, and continued to stare at the house. He knew as well as I did that this wasn't right.

'We move on,' he said, and we went back to the machine gun crew and told them to shoulder their weapon. We were going to explore further, to see if we could find out anything of use. We left the target house untouched and pressed on into

Daesh territory. The lack of life meant that the operation had turned from a hit-and-run sniper mission into a reconnaissance patrol.

We swung in a loop so as to approach a village a further two kilometres on from the south, the opposite direction from which they would expect an attack. We snuck up as quietly as possible and, once again, set up watching through our scopes, looking for any sign of life at all. It was quite a large village and we'd have expected to see something: a chicken, a cat, anything. But nothing stirred.

It may sound strange, but the eerie stillness made the whole patrol even more stressful. The complete absence of any life, except for the ever-present rodents scuttling in the grass, just seemed utterly unnatural. It certainly had us worried.

We had been out much longer than anticipated and had covered far more ground. We had to head back quickly, or else risk getting caught out in the open between our lines and the enemy as the sun came up. We still had the problem of the erratic terrain and moving faster meant that all of us took tumbles in the dark. But by four in the morning we staggered back into our base and the welcoming arms of our comrades, who had steaming sweet tea and food ready for us. We were all exhausted but the general in command of the area wanted our report immediately, and she got it in between mouthfuls of salty cheese and gulps of chai.

Our finding nothing but empty positions caused some comment and confusion. We had logged our progress with a GPS and a tablet with a mapping app, and went through the various logged trenches and fortifications with SDF intelligence. As to where Daesh were, the conclusions drawn were that they were either dug into tunnels for the night and so keeping right out of view – although then we would have expected to at least see signs of sentries – or else they were not actively holding the terrain and were just making a lot of noise with their rockets to disguise their weakness.

This raised some ideas in my head. If Daesh weren't guarding this terrain it gave us the opportunity to do some damage to them.

Speaking to the YPJ general, I aired a suggestion.

'What we should do is send a sabotage and sniper party out at night and mine one of the areas we know their rocket crews use. The sabotage guys can go back and the snipers, with a Zagros and a Dragunov, can lie up in the grass, say eight hundred metres away, and watch,' I told her. 'If one of the Daesh sets off the mine, we wait and watch the ones who come to investigate. Then we shoot the leader and as many of their followers as we can.'

'Why do you think a leader would come?' she asked.

I shrugged, then said:

'When a mine goes off over here you go and investigate with your people to find out what happened. They probably do the same.'

'The snipers will be out in the open and exposed,' she countered.

'Two snipers in the grass, with range on their side? That is not something anyone in their right mind wants to face. Besides, we can tell the Americans our plan. If Daesh come after the snipers with a lot of troops, the Americans are itching for a target like that. Lots of Daesh out in the open? They'll kill them all.'

The YPJ general looked thoughtful.

'That's a good tactic. I like it. I shall talk it over with my commander.'

Despite her positive response the plan was written off as too ambitious by high command. Fair enough. Instead, more patrols were dispatched and this culminated in a strong patrol going out a few nights later and actively exploring some buildings in Daesh territory, then hitting another with an RPG. Looking back, I suspect that our policy was to try to draw Daesh troops to hold the territory, thus draining them from other areas.

Certainly our activities and aggressive night patrols caused a response, and we had a drone appear over us again on the 5th. The snipers were on active guard at the time, as other units were holding tac mils and had asked us to cover their shift. As a result we picked up on the intruder rapidly and it got a hot reception, all of us blasting away with various small arms to drive it off, which it did sharply when it realised we had been all but waiting for it. I cursed not having a machine gun; a PKM with some tracers and we could knock these pests out of the sky.

The reason for our visitor became apparent that night. At 0130 we got an alert, and one serious enough to get even me out of bed. Daesh had sent six suicide vehicles in a massed attack against us. The good news was that if we found the terrain difficult to negotiate during our night patrols, the drivers of the VBIEDs, entombed in their armoured boxes with nothing but narrow slots to look through, found it impossible. We watched, breath held, as the ominous vehicles drove around in circles, occasionally flicking on a light to try to find a target.

We all kept silent and watched, as any sort of fire would draw their attention.

Unfortunately, one of the neighbouring Asayish positions got spooked and fired a burst of tracer in the VBIEDs' general direction. Lights came on and swung around towards the Asayish, who luckily were several kilometres away, well out of the drivers' view, and sensibly stopped shooting. They were also helped by a burst of fire from another position even further away. The VBIEDs continued to rove around in no man's land, seeking a target but finding nothing. As the sun rose we prepared ourselves for the vehicles to finally catch sight of us, but they instead seemed to be trying to disguise themselves from coalition aircraft or else had managed to get themselves stuck in the myriad holes and wadis on the plain. A high-altitude aircraft appeared and proceeded to meticulously destroy the vehicles.

That seemed that, but Daesh thought they wouldn't let us off completely and hit the village with a rocket. They really were being quite tiresome.

10

In Qamishli, Watching the Turks Destroy Nusaybin, Training

May 2016

After nearly a month at the front my sniper team was replaced and we returned to Sari Kani for a welcome chance to have a rest without the threat of being rocketed or facing a VBIED. The Turkish tanks that sat a couple of miles away continued to point their cannons directly at us, and the wall the Turks were building along the border was rapidly approaching completion on this stretch. Hozan had completed his six months, so headed back to Canada, but things were far from quiet. Moe and Curly had managed to wangle a transfer to the snipers, and a number of other tabors had been transferred to the area around our base, meaning a daily stream of visitors, among them my old friend Kemal; Akif the leatherneck, a former US Marine who had become Inbred's battle buddy and was a solid presence when in action; Roza, a young girl from

Sweden who had come to Rojava just before me and proved a lot more committed to the fight in Syria than some of the Rambo types that had passed through; and Givara, a skinny, good-natured British farmer.

The news constantly reported on the fighting in Turkey, where the Turkish army was alleged to be destroying city after city. The Kurds started a training regime – again, mainly their ideological sessions, but some of them actually began running in the morning! Moe and Curly were in high demand to teach first aid to the other tabors and I went along to pick up what I could and help out where needed. We tried to get ourselves and the Kurds as ready as possible for whatever was to come next. It duly arrived, and from an unexpected angle.

The Assad regime and the YPG had long had an uneasy peace. Assad's men held districts in Hasakah and Qamishli, and things normally ticked along fine, with both sides maintaining a truce while they dealt with bigger issues. Certain segments of the Western media suggested this represented an alliance between the two parties. I can assure you it did not. I cannot speak for the regime's attitude, but the YPG held Assad in contempt. He was, after all, the epitome of the sort of divisive dictator that their ideological structure had been formed to oppose. The general feeling was that peace was fine for the moment, but no one doubted a reckoning was due at some point. With that level of tension, outbreaks of hostilities were inevitable. In late April there was fighting in Qamishli between forces loyal to Assad and the YPG. Though it was quickly resolved, tensions remained high and, as a result, a battle group was assembled to present a show of strength to the regime and deter further aggression. I was part of the sniper detachment.

Though I'd passed through Qamishli many times I hadn't spent any significant time in the city and was interested to see more. Our position was on the outskirts, overlooking the airport, which was in regime hands and from which Hind attack helicopters and MIG fighters took off routinely, quite often to circle threateningly overhead. In the event of conflict, we snipers were to use our Zagros heavy rifles to close the airport, shooting anything that tried to take off. We positioned ourselves on a high building, which gave a good view of the runway and terminal. It also gave a good view the other way, into the city of Nusaybin, just over the border in Turkey. The two cities were essentially one, divided by the drawing of the border line. And though Nusaybin had always been the wealthier city thanks to Turkey's larger economy, leaving Qamishli to look rather shabby in comparison to its conjoined twin, that was no longer the case.

During my time in Syria I saw huge levels of destruction. I saw entire neighbourhoods wrecked by Daesh booby traps. I saw hundreds (thousands?) of coalition airstrikes, everything from heavy bombing to areas drenched by the fire of an AC-130. But I have never seen anything like the destruction that the Turks were wreaking on one of their own cities. Nusaybin wasn't just burning. It was being systematically obliterated.

For three days I watched as heavy artillery marched up and down the town in waves that must have been like the 'marching fire' used in the First World War. But this wasn't a military front line; it was a civilian city. The only time the rain of shells and mortars seemed to stop was to allow aircraft to swoop in. The Phantom and F-16 jets didn't drop precision munitions, as I was used to seeing out here. They carpet-bombed the houses. The destruction was incredible.

Nusaybin, with a largely Kurdish population, had experienced an uprising in November 2015 after months of protests in response to the Turkish army destroying Kurdish towns across the east and south of the country following the collapse of talks the previous July, and an ad hoc militia had formed to protect the residents from the army's depredations. The Turkish military had responded by imposing curfews and, as their grip slipped, finally resorted to a state of siege in March 2016. This went on for four months, ending in July. I'm amazed the rebels held as long as they did. In May, it didn't look like there was much left to fight over!

It was, in a word, horrifying. Some people ask me if I have issues with what I did and saw in Syria. I can safely say no. I did nothing there that bothers me, or brings me regret. But I am sometimes woken up in the night by dreams of bombs falling on Nusaybin.

What really got to me was the low level of coverage that the situation received in the Western press, despite every volunteer who passed through Rojava taking away with them a deep anger at the Erdoğan regime, which they expounded upon at length to anyone who would listen. I have lost count of the number of volunteers' complaints I have heard about interviews being given to the media, only to have any criticisms of the Turkish regime omitted from the broadcast – this happened constantly. Yet I suppose one shouldn't be too surprised. Turkey has in the last hundred years committed several bouts of genocide and ethnic cleansing against a variety of its minorities; when a country acts in such a way in such a comparatively short period of time, it isn't an anomaly, it's a policy. To paraphrase Stalin, if a country commits a genocide, it is castigated. If it commits three or four no one can remember if it's three, or four.

The death throes of Nusaybin were a contrast to events on our side of the border, where peace, though uneasy, reigned. It soon became apparent that Assad's troops had heeded the warning signalled by our mass deployment, and we returned to Sari Kani to continue training. In our absence, Moe and Curly had been busy planning an effective programme that would include weapon and house clearance drills as well as providing first aid training to any SDF tabor that requested it – of which there was never a shortage. Because so many tabors were now circulating in the area there were always training sessions going on, and we started seeing SDF units actually undertaking their own field exercises and clearance practice.

Our ammunition situation had improved dramatically, and we now had a large surplus that allowed more extravagant use while honing our skills. We had the proper sniper bullets to go with the Dragunovs, something that had been exceedingly rare in the past. We also received quantities of brand new bullets for the Kalashnikovs and Zagros rifles. These were to cause some amusement. Our ammunition had always been of old Warsaw Pact or Chinese origin and came in the heavy metal cans that were a standard feature of these producers. These new bullets – beautifully made with brass cases as opposed to the usual rough steel we were used to – came in pristine white card boxes with crisp printing on them in English. They quite clearly stated the ammunition they contained and had *Made in Russia* distinctly marked. They would also have a long and elaborate safety warning on the back, concerning the dangers of lead poisoning and the need to be sure to wash any residue off your hands after use. It was this that caused comment. The Russians are not renowned for being particularly concerned with health and safety, nor for bothering to get their English translations utterly perfect on their products. The health warning smacked of Western legal regulations being applied to their fullest.

The 12.7mm ammunition also caused comment. It came in the same white packaging as the AK ammunition, five bullets to a box. It was all full metal jacket – a standard military bullet, in other words. This wasn't particularly popular as we preferred armour-piercing incendiary or, even better, full explosive rounds in the Zagros. The reason for this was that with the Zagros we were unlikely to be aiming for a single individual (though, of course, it did occur), but rather for an area target like a house, bunker or vehicle. As a result, the extra penetration and the explosive charge were far more effective than a straight lead bullet. The explosion also made spotting the fall of shot easier, an issue when firing to the sort of ranges we would use the Zagros at. But we were happy to at least have new and well-made ammunition, and in quantities that would allow us to be even more effective.

The amusing factor with the new 12.7mm bullets – other than the statutory health warning – was another detail marked on the boxes. Under the inscription *12.7x108mm Full Metal*

Jacket was *Hunting Bullets*. This caused me to ask what exactly we were supposed to be hunting with these monstrous rounds. Tyrannosaurus Rex?

With this bounty of ammunition we tried to conduct the most effective practice possible. As the Kurds were still dismissive of Western tactics it was just Moe, Curly and me from the sniper tabor, joined by Akif, Inbred and Roza, whose tabors were still housed nearby. Under Moe and Curly's tutelage we practised weapons handling, emergency drills, marksmanship and team house clearances with live ammunition. One exercise required four men to breach a house while I provided sniper support. I needed to hit targets in two separate rooms to initiate the exercise. This would require me to shoot only a metre over the heads of the assault teams.

This was a classic case of training being more stressful than combat and, as a result, preparing you somewhat for the difficulties you face. Though in reality an easy shot, the thought of possibly hitting a friend really puts the pressure on you. Which is, as I say, why you train. Fortunately the exercise, which included the use of a live grenade, went off perfectly.

As our skills improved we would invite members of the SDF to come and witness these practice sessions. The idea was to get them to adopt basic training methods, so as to improve their effectiveness in the campaign that we all knew was coming, and reduce casualties. Though the SDF were brave, the general standard of military skill was very low, and even those who had seen combat still had the disconcerting habit of closing their eyes when they shot, or else holding their rifles above their heads when firing from cover.

We received a lot of favourable feedback on these

demonstrations and, had there been time, perhaps a decent basic training programme could have been instituted. But time was against us: soon we would be off on campaign again. And this would be a much bloodier affair.

11

Manbij

June 2016

The next phase in the war on Daesh was going to be by far the most complex operation undertaken by the SDF at that time. We had originally expected to attack Jarabulus, a town across the Euphrates on the Syrian-Turkish border that was used as the main conduit in the trade between ISIS and Turkey. If we could take this, then Daesh's main supply corridor to their backers in the wider world would be cut. The SDF, or more specifically the Kurds of the YPG, hoped that taking Jarabulus would enable a further drive across the north of Syria that would allow Rojava to link up with the Kurdish-majority canton of Afrin. As the vast majority of the YPG, and its best equipment, was located in Afrin, uniting the two districts would free up considerable resources. Unfortunately, politics would intrude.

The Erdoğan government had made all too plain that the Kurdish issue was their primary concern in the region, and that under no circumstances would they tolerate any move by the SDF against Jarabulus, or indeed across the Euphrates. Although Turkey would later engage in operations against the Islamic State in August 2016, and start to suffer terrorist outrages at their hands, there was no doubt in any of our minds that the Erdoğan regime was a primary supporter of Daesh through trade: anyone who had served across from Jarabulus, or any other vantage point on the river front, could see the heavy truck traffic passing over the border.

As we were told in our pre-operation briefing (judge the reliability of that as you choose), the US had told Turkey that if they wanted to stop the SDF from crossing the Euphrates with American support, they would have to take action to remove the border territory from ISIS control and place another suitable faction in charge of the region. They were given a six-month timeframe in which to achieve this. When it didn't happen, the SDF got the green light to launch their own invasion. Jarabulus was considered far too controversial to attack: any SDF attempt on the town would no doubt be the spark for a Turkish invasion. Instead another target, one that would cut the Daesh capital of Raqqa off from Turkey and disrupt the illegal oil trade that was funding their war effort, was necessary. The logical one was Manbij. The city, sitting thirty kilometres from the west bank of the Euphrates, was a critical communications nexus for ISIS, and a crossroads for northern Syria, linking Raqqa to Jarabulus and Turkey. Its capture would be a major blow for Daesh.

The Battle of Manbij was a major undertaking for the SDF. Although I cannot be sure of the specifics, as I was not sitting around in some command centre making strategy, we were told that the SDF would launch a four-pronged attack across the Euphrates, which would allow us to encircle the city, cut off the critical roads providing Raqqa with its northern supply route and demonstrate that the SDF, at least, was committed to driving ISIS out of Syria.

A plan was implemented to disguise our objective. From 20 May the Kobane Brigade of the YPG and its local SDF allies started pushing south and attacking the villages that made up the front towards Raqqa itself. Coalition aircraft also started dropping leaflets warning residents to leave the city. At the same time, in Iraq, the reconstituted Iraqi army and the Kurdish Peshmergas began putting pressure on Fallujah and Mosul. With so many points under attack, the idea was to push Daesh reserves and confuse them as to our actual target.

On the 26th we moved into action. A huge convoy, containing all of the prime units of the Mobile Brigade and additional forces from the other regional brigades, started to form up and move out. As we rumbled through Rojava people swarmed out of their houses to stare at the procession, which stretched for miles as more tabors joined. It was the greatest display of military strength that northern Syria had seen since the start of the civil war.

The mood was jubilant as we rolled through the countryside. We had been waiting to really hit the enemy for months, and now we were on the march. The column turned south long before we reached the Euphrates, and followed the road leading to Raqqa. This was part of our deception plan. Daesh would know that we were moving – there was no way to disguise such a force – and they still had some sympathisers among the civilian population. But we could keep Daesh guessing until we struck.

As we passed through villages that only days before had been held by ISIS, we started seeing the destruction wrought by the recent airstrikes. Though this was hardly rare in the areas further north, once people came back into a liberated area the damage would generally start to be repaired, and in some towns it wasn't rare for such reconstruction to remove any sign of the war. But one of the villages in particular that we stopped in caught my attention. The whole place had been levelled down to the bedrock. Such destruction was rare; normally you would see one building destroyed but those around it untouched.

An SDF trooper I was talking to saw my confusion and looked around to see what it was that had caught my attention.

'This was an airstrike?' I asked. 'Big airstrike!'

He scanned the devastation and turned back to me with a grin and an answer.

'Ah,' he said. 'Russians.'

The column stopped at one of the huge grain silo complexes that dot the landscape of northern Syria. These make useful military bases as they have plenty of room for vehicles to park, a particular problem when you have several low-loaders carrying tanks, let alone a range of other trucks and cars. This complex also stood by a crossroads; one road went to the Euphrates, another to Raqqa. Here we stopped and waited for our jump off. We were close enough to the front line that Daesh was able to rocket us on occasion, and Moe found he suddenly had employment as a medic again when one Katyusha screamed in and impacted on a government building in which some local defence forces were stationed. One trooper had cause to be thankful for the stout construction of such buildings, when the rocket hit the roof directly above his bunk. The result was a large chunk of concrete coming down on his head and a trip to hospital after Moe had treated him, but better that than having the rocket explode in the barracks.

The local forces that garrisoned the silos, standing around in awe of the mass of firepower that had rolled in on them for a visit, had a powerful thermal scope mounted at the top of the depository to watch for any spoiling attack that ISIS might launch against us. Any attempt would be swift suicide, but Daesh never were scared of dying.

We received our briefing from the head of the YPG and settled down to wait. On 29 May units started to move out, and by the 31st our battle group had settled into a small town overlooking the Euphrates. Coalition airpower was hammering anything that moved, as well as any suspected defensive positions on the other side of the river. We were tense with expectation. The bridge here had been blown up early in the conflict and it was apparent that we would have to force a river crossing against a dug-in enemy, never a manoeuvre to be undertaken lightly.

Moe gave me a handful of syringes that he had prefilled with a variety of painkillers, and briefed me on how to use them. He and Curly, with a few members of the sniper tabor, were in the first wave that would go across in RIBs being operated by American Special Forces. This wave would have to grab the steep hills on the far side of the river and drive out any resistance.

As night fell and the time approached for the first wave to go over, the coalition really upped the ante on their fire support. A Special Forces mortar team started bombarding the hills, firing dozens of bombs and plastering the other side of the river. They were joined by fighter jets that screamed overhead and comprehensively blasted the opposite bank, and then came an AC-130 gunship, which sat overhead and mowed countless rounds into the slopes to suppress any sort of resistance. To say it was impressive doesn't do it justice.

The heavy drenching with ordnance meant that our first wave were able to get across and take their objectives, though even saturation with such firepower didn't stop Daesh entirely. There was some fighting with scattered and disorganised combatants, and the light of the following day would see them make attempts to shell the crossing point on multiple occasions. However, they had lost the river hilltops to the SDF and weren't able to land their projectiles with any accuracy.

On 2 June I went across. American Special Forces had dug up an ancient Soviet pontoon ferry, no doubt out of some Syrian army desert scrapyard, and were using it to laboriously transport our army across the Euphrates. As it could only manage about fifteen vehicles at a time, it was going to take several days more to get the vast backlog of units across and into the attack.

The crossing point was at the destroyed Qere Qozag Bridge. SDF diggers had cut approaches from the road down the steep banks to the river, which would serve as our embarkation points. Diggers were also working on the bridge, dropping spoil into the river to fill the gaps in the spans. It would be a primitive and short-lived repair, but would get the bridge operational for long enough to allow our supplies to reach us from Rojava.

It was, however, apparent that the SDF, always eager to get into action, were going to make things more complicated through impatience. The Americans were trying to keep the queue to the side of the roads, maintaining a clear lane for any traffic, principally ambulances with wounded, making the return trip, and as an access point for any priority vehicles that had need to cross at the earliest opportunity. Unfortunately, for the SDF an empty space leading to the front of the line simply signalled an opportunity to barge in. As a result a stream of vehicles, all sounding their horns continuously, jostled for position in a desperate attempt to get across. It was utter chaos.

The Americans dealing with the traffic were pulling their hair out. As soon as they got one vehicle out of the way another simply dived in. As it was plain that we weren't going anywhere, I offered what assistance I could and headed to the rear of the queue to get them to back up and pull over onto the verges. It was while I was doing this that one of the YPG generals pulled up and, seeing me standing in the middle of the road leaning on my rifle as an impromptu roadblock, couldn't resist a joke.

'Botan! I didn't know there were snipers in the Asayish,' he laughed.

'Funny. Where are the Asayish? They should be doing this.'

He pointed at some of the vehicles that, now my back was turned, were trying to sneak down to the front.

'They want to get across,' he grinned.

I tried, I really did, but it was a classic example of trying to herd cats. After two hours of cajoling, negotiation, threats and tantrums – all from the SDF, I wasn't going to rise to any of it – I'd had enough. I went up to the US guys at the crossing point.

'Sorry lads, I've done all I can, but it's just going to get worse.'

'It's OK, thanks for helping. At least we got the tanks across with your help – that was the priority,' I was told. Knowing how limited our tanks could be, I thought that perhaps high command's priorities might have been a bit askew, but tanks do look the part and if Daesh attacked the landing point in force, having a bit of heavy armour that side of the river should give them pause.

My help didn't go unrewarded.

'Get your vehicles up here, we'll clear a spot and get you across as soon as we can.'

It took another hour, during which we suffered long and loud complaints about our getting a modicum of preferential treatment. But the tabor's YPJ second-in-command, for whom I was acting as driver on the crossing, gave short shrift to those who complained. She was renowned as a steely-eyed killer throughout the SDF, and a sharp glance from her would make anyone retreat.

We drove along the valley road that led from the river and turned off into a camp spot in the forested hills, where I was to find Moe and Curly waiting. The position, straight up a steep track, would protect us from any attempt to use a VBIED against us and the trees gave us cover from observation. However, Daesh knew we were across and intended to welcome us; we received regular rocketing from some keen type who would shoot four projectiles at once. The grove that we laagered up in had irrigation channels dug through it, only about nine inches to a foot deep, but by scraping them out further and sleeping in them we avoided any casualties as Mr Four Rocket, as I named him, dropped his ordnance across the slopes. And this was no mild threat, as he did a pretty good job of regularly hitting our position, missing Curly by scant metres just before I met up with them.

The SDF consolidated its bridgehead and pushed further into the hills so that by 3 June we were looking down on the plains. I found myself stationed with Curly and Moe on a lone rocky peak, which was serving as the forward command post for my battlegroup commander and her staff. It gave me an excellent view across the flat ground and towns and villages that stretched before us. It was so good a position as to be obvious that the SDF would use it, and Mr Four Rockets made a number of spirited attempts to hit us. On several occasions his trademark salvo whistled down to make impact on the hillside or the surrounding fields. Once, a gaggle of civilians, perhaps thirty or forty, mainly women and children, were passing to get away from ISIS-held ground when the distinctive *whoosh* came. I could tell from the sound that the projectiles were headed for these people below. I watched in horror, expecting to have to rush down the sheer sides to give assistance to any casualties, but unbelievably the rockets bracketed the group in a neat diamond formation and injured none of them! Mr Four Rockets' luck finally ran out that afternoon, when he was found out in the open by a coalition aircraft.

We had just settled down for lunch on the hilltop when someone started yelling and gunfire erupted below us. The SDF had been moving to take one of the villages at the base of the hills when a vanload of Daesh had suddenly appeared – a bad mistake for them, as not only did they have to face the troops in front of them but the array of dushkas on the hill. And us.

Moe, Curly and I began shooting, though the range was about twelve hundred metres and on the extreme end of my Dragunov's capability. However, Moe on the Zagros was able to hit the truck cleanly, which set it on fire. As the SDF moved in we watched them chase the enemy into the village and wipe them out.

The excitement wasn't over yet. Back at the campsite in the hill groves, an alert went out that a suicide vehicle was barrelling down the main road towards the bridge and would pass below where we were camped. The whole camp ran down the hill with whatever weapons were on hand to try and stop the VBIED and, as it rounded the corner about five hundred metres from us, a dushka managed to hit it hard enough to stop it dead, but the beast did not explode. It just sat there. We didn't know if it had been fully immobilised or not, if the driver was still alive or if he was now just looking for a target. The dushka crew, after bouncing several shells off the vehicle's thick armour, decided that they were getting out while the going was good and left us scratching our heads as to what to do. No one would go near it, as it was obviously at the higher end of the VBIEDs used by Daesh and would carry a huge amount of explosive, and we had no anti-armour weapons apart from RPGs, which no one was willing to get close enough to use. Moe and I eventually set off to fetch a Zagros, so he could try to kill the damn thing. We were just heading back when something screamed right over our heads, followed by a massive explosion. At first we thought that we had been hit by an errant airstrike, but then, as bits of steel started to fall from the heavens, it became apparent that the coalition had dealt with our problem for us. We were thankful, even if it did mean rolling back into the irrigation scrapes and waiting for the raining debris to stop.

The day had been busy enough, but was to be a foretaste of what was going to be an extremely hectic night. As night fell I was called forward and told I would be accompanying a night attack with an infantry tabor. The partner assigned to me was one of the more experienced fighters, though only twenty-five, and I knew I could rely on him. Our job was to lead the unit across country to seize a village that would be the start of our breakout from the hills near the river, out into the rolling farm country and olive groves that stretched all the way to Manbij. He would lead with an M16 equipped with a thermal to scout the way while I would back him up with my Kalashnikov. I would also be carrying my Dragunov as we would have to defend what we took the next day from any Daesh counterattack.

The unit mustered up and we headed out at 2200. A slow and painstaking march over two kilometres in the pitch black followed, with my partner stopping regularly to make long sweeps of our surroundings. There were units moving through the night to seize other objectives, and we had to be as careful not to run across them in the dark as we were to not get caught in an ISIS ambush. It took us two hours to reach the objective. We quietly approached, and then rushed the first house in our line of advance.

We found a family sleeping on the roof and while the unit secured the immediate area, the commander and his Arabic speaker tried to talk to them as they huddled together. This hit a problem as they didn't seem to speak that language. Various dialects and other languages were tried with no success. I was crouched behind the roof parapet, listening rather than watching for the enemy when the father asked the interpreter:

'Do you speak English?'

'I do,' I said, to the consternation of my SDF colleagues. None of them did and there promptly ensued a discussion whether or not I should talk to this man. I suspect their concerns were that I might glean some critical information that I would not want to share with YPG intelligence, which I had no intention of doing. So I resolved the issue by ignoring them, squatting down in front of the man and getting on with it anyway.

He and his family were Nigerians who had come to Syria for, he said, the purpose of building houses.

This caused me to pause.

'You came here to build houses?!'

'Yes.'

'You came to Syria, to a warzone, to ISIS, to build houses?! And you brought your family?!!'

'Yes.'

It was too dark to see his face to judge his expression but his voice sounded unsure. Though it must be extremely disconcerting to be woken in the middle of the night to find yourself surrounded by armed men and women, I would have put serious money on him lying through his teeth.

'What's he saying?' asked the tabor commander.

I straightened up.

'He says he builds houses,' I replied.

'Here?! He came to Daesh with his family to build houses?!' Evidently I wasn't the only one to think this unlikely.

'I think he is Boko Haram,' I said. 'We need to give him to the Asayish and intelligence for questioning.'

'Boko Haram? *No boş*. He must go to intelligence.'

Guards were detailed to hold the family until reinforcements came up, and we slipped off into the night once again. We infiltrated the centre of the village before once again storming a rooftop to secure a building that would be suitable as a command post and sniper point.

This also proved to be occupied, with almost twenty women and children of various ages. Here the advantage of having YPJ fighters in the unit really showed. The brief shrieks from the startled civilians were soon reduced to confused chatter as the women fighters reassured them that they were not under threat and that we were here to keep them safe. When they found out that we were SDF the civilians got positively enthusiastic about our presence. As many of them were Kurds, that is understandable.

The presence of the women and kids gave us a serious problem. We couldn't let them go because, despite their claiming to be glad to see us, we couldn't be sure they wouldn't immediately rush to any Daesh in the area and inform them of our presence. We also didn't want them wandering around in the dark because a firefight could erupt at any moment, with them caught in the middle of it. However, keeping them on the roof meant that if a fight did start they could be in serious danger, especially if a suicide vehicle was used against us.

The commanders made their decision. The civilians would stay with us and we would have to take every measure to protect them. So the YPJ settled them down into the corner furthest from likely contact and we set about fortifying the roof and waiting for any reaction from Daesh.

About three in the morning, we got one. Machine gun fire ripped across the night sky as one of the other SDF units, slipping through the night, alerted a Daesh sentry and a firefight of utter confusion ensued. The intention is to shoot the enemy, but when it is so dark you can't even see your own sights, let alone the building they are firing from, it's more a case of lining up on a muzzle flash and firing in return. It's largely a waste without tracers – shooting in these conditions means most aim high without realising it – and I only had about one per AK magazine, which I would normally load fourth from the bottom so that I would know when to change the magazine. Unfortunately, most were so old they didn't burn visibly anyway. Regardless, you add your weight to the fire: if you can't kill the enemy you can convince him to bugger off.

The other, much more pressing, concern in a fight like this is target confusion. In the pitch black with nothing but blazing muzzle flashes to shoot at, it is easy to get turned about and lose track of where friendly units are. An almost tragic example of this happened that night. As we fired at the enemy, a unit located on a roof off on our left flank mistook us for the enemy and let rip with a long burst from a machine gun straight into our rooftop. The first I was aware of a problem was when a stream of tracer tore into the inside of the parapet wall behind me with an awful racket, only a metre to the side of a woman fighter who was shooting at Daesh. She screamed and wisely rolled into a ball on the floor as the tracer pinged in random directions, and the rest of us rapidly followed suit. If the machine-gunner started walking his fire across our rooftop we were completely exposed.

Fortunately the squad commander got control of the situation by roaring the most abusive invective over the radio at the errant gunner, who stopped shooting. Bad language, even raising your voice, is deeply frowned upon in the YPG, but everyone was in agreement that this was definitely an occasion that warranted it. How we didn't suffer any casualties is a mystery to me, especially as a large section of the roof was covered with women and children lying on mattresses.

And how were our hosts faring, in the middle of what was turning into a savage firefight? They were loving it! They kept up a constant stream of commentary as they tried to sit up far enough to watch the action while staying low enough not to get shot. They would periodically cheer and applaud when one of our tracers whizzed close enough to a Daesh muzzle flash to get him to stop firing. In fact, they acted exactly like a crowd of supporters at a sports match, a thoroughly bizarre situation.

It occurred to me, as the battle wound down and Daesh took to their heels, that the attitude of civilians during my time in the conflict zone had changed remarkably. During my first operation, Sarrin in July 2015, the civilians pretty much all fled our advance, either into Daesh territory or else to other cities well away from the fighting. The towns we fought in were deserted and stayed so for months afterwards. During the Al Hawl offensive in November 2015, civilians would run towards us and through our lines, and then camp just behind the front. People would even come and complain after a few days that we were not moving forwards fast enough and they wanted to go home! By Shaddadi in February 2016, they would largely stay in place and, in the event of a fight, would retreat to a safe(ish) distance to watch us and Daesh slug it out. And now here they were, treating it like a game of football!

I was exhausted after being on the go for so long, but I had to knock holes in the parapet so that I could set my Dragunov to cover the road for the coming day. This accomplished, I settled myself down and fought not to fall asleep as I lay behind my rifle and watched the road through my scope. As ever, we had to expect a suicide attack. The road came into my view about eight hundred metres away and then curved to our left at seven hundred metres. That is what I set my scope reticule at, as a vehicle would then present its side to me for some distance as it ran in to the village we held. I would shoot for tyres if attacked and had a good expectation of achieving hits. Because the road didn't run directly at us we could engage anything on it and still be able to clear the roof before the vehicle could turn into our part of town and head towards us. Daesh knew we were here. They knew this was our breakout from the hills. They were likely to try to stop us.

At 0530, just after dawn, a figure appeared on the road and came wandering down towards us.

'A man,' I called to my partner who, having switched his thermal scope for an ACOG-style sight, observed our visitor alongside me.

'He's carrying a child.'

I looked closely at the target. He did indeed have a bundle in his arms that he was carrying like it was a baby. But the bundle was wrapped in a tarpaulin.

'I don't think it's a child,' I said. 'You don't wrap babies in plastic.'

He grunted in agreement.

'At three hundred metres I will shoot warning shot,' he said.

The man continued to wander down the road without a care in the world. I watched his face closely. Everyone in the area would know that there had been a battle in the night and that the SDF were here. His expression was fixed and he never looked at us, not even a glance. By now he also had more than a dozen troopers watching his every move.

My partner took careful aim and squeezed off a round.

I had observed that people in Syria who got shot at reacted in three distinct ways. Civilians would normally continue on regardless, oblivious to the fact someone was shooting at them, or they would raise their hands and look completely astonished that anyone could consider them worth shooting.

People expecting trouble, such as fighters, would react with alacrity and either return fire or go for cover.

This guy went for cover. 'Baby' was cast aside and he lit off at a heck of a rate, in a zigzag. Most worryingly, he did it towards us. With no obvious weapon to hand this could only mean one thing. He was wearing a suicide vest.

A small house, little more than a shack, stood between us and he was able, with commendable speed, to reach the protection it provided, despite my, and my various colleagues', efforts, which had sent a storm of fire his way as soon as he ran. But he was now stuck. To get to us, his target, he would have to charge across five hundred metres of open ground with a now thoroughly alerted enemy waiting for him. To make the point, I put a few rounds into the edge of the building where he was hiding. The gratifying spray of dirt from these would let him know that any attempt to close on us would be a failure.

A standoff ensued. We all stayed glued to the house, weapons at shoulders, waiting for him to make his move. The minutes ticked away and nothing moved. As the sun was well up, the tabor commander told the women that they should go below and perhaps think about moving away from us as the suicide bomber might just be the start of an attack. They refused, and insisted on staying to watch us in action. Some of the younger girls were ordered to go and fetch us tea as guests. The bomber still hadn't moved when it arrived and I lay at my murder hole glued to my scope, muttering my thanks as a child put a glass of sweet tea at my elbow. It gradually cooled as I continued to watch.

And then he broke cover. He evidently thought better of trying to come at us and ran back towards a house on the bend of the road. If he could make it he would be safe from us, and able either to escape or wait for us to advance and jump one of our units at close range. A blizzard of fire from the infantry chased him as he once again zigzagged towards safety. I waited, trying to judge when he was going to switch direction and, just as he was approaching the house that would protect him, squeezed the trigger. I fired a fraction of a second after the other sniper.

The man dropped and lay on the ground. He was only five metres from the house that he had been heading for. I couldn't tell which of us had hit him, perhaps both, but a threat had been dealt with and we both relaxed. I drank my cold tea.

'He is moving,' shouted the sentry.

I slid back behind my gun and looked through the scope. The guy had rolled onto his back and was waving his arm slowly in the air.

There followed a hurried discussion on what to do and the commander decided to send out a patrol. Three men went out and approached cautiously. When they got 150 metres from him they started shouting at him to show his hands clearly. He continued to wave for them to come over to him. The patrol got more aggressive and rifles were shouldered and aimed. If he couldn't prove he wasn't a threat he was going to get shot again. I must admit a doubt appeared in my mind. Had we actually just gunned down a civilian?

Then he exploded.

Perhaps he decided that enough was enough and he wasn't going to have any success in killing any of us, so what the heck. Perhaps the bullets had caused some damage to the ignition system. It doesn't really matter. All I know was that it was a hell of a blast.

The patrol were blown flat by the shock wave and, after we had picked ourselves up, we watched anxiously to see if any of them were injured. They pulled themselves out the dirt and, after checking for injuries, dusted each other off before heading over to our unlamented foe. There was nothing left of him but a few scraps of cloth, fluttering in the breeze.

The rest of the morning was spent on alert, which gradually wound down as other SDF units leapfrogged past us to take the rest of the town and continue the drive on Manbij. Our hosts widely applauded us for the entertainment and then proceeded to feed us and maintain a near-continuous stream of water and chai. The kids took squealing delight in running around the roof, collecting our spent brass and staring in awe at our weapons. I was singled out for some hardcore goggling when someone told them I was an Englishman who had come to fight Daesh for them. We headed out in the afternoon, leaving our gracious hosts to wave us off and call the blessings of Allah down upon us.

The next day brought the chance for a rest, though even that was relative as we were mortared several times. I was also able to help get a sick child evacuated to get medical attention. Then on 6 June it was back into the fight proper. Our infantry had advanced against a village that morning and hit resistance, including a sniper. As a result a group of us were rushed in to support them and remove the threat.

The fight was rumbling on when we arrived, and I set up my position and started watching. There were a number of Daesh fighters engaging the SDF, who had gradually been pushed back, and reports still kept coming in that a sniper was operating and that he was inflicting casualties. This was who I wanted. I scanned the few buildings that Daesh still held, waiting for him to either move or shoot. Something caught my eye, something protruding from a window. A long barrel. It was a long way out, at least a kilometre, but he was lining up for his own shot and, even if I couldn't be sure of taking him out, I could stop him from shooting any more of my comrades. I squeezed the trigger. But someone beat me to it.

A sudden flash dazzled me through my scope and I was treated to a spectacular sight. The entire base of the house, a large two-storey structure, was boiling with flame. The whole building seemed to rise into the air on a column of fire, where it then turned a slow cartwheel before crashing down to earth.

I lifted my head away from my scope and stared up. An A-10, obviously the responsible party, howled overhead through the smoke of the destruction it had wrought before banking sharply and triggering off a deafening long salvo from its cannon into a group of Daesh that were beyond my sight line. A cheer went up and that was the end of resistance. The A10 had exterminated the whole group in two runs.

The approach to Manbij slowed to a crawl as Daesh fought us for every little village and town. The SDF fought hard, and casualties mounted. The fighting escalated rapidly as we pushed deeper into Daesh territory. And Daesh were constantly working to counter us. On the 8th I spent a frantic few hours with the French Special Forces team trying to find a drone that was buzzing around overhead. These guys had evidently taken as deep a dislike to the things as I had, and though we could hear it we never did spot it.

A few days later Daesh showed what their high-flying reconnaissance had been looking at. On the 11th they launched a night assault at several points on our advance in an attempt to cut off our entire spearhead from our supply line across the river. A ferocious battle developed, and was only turned around by the coalition's heavy use of airpower. At least one Asayish unit was overrun and wiped out to a man. Daesh managed to suppress them on the rooftop where they had been sleeping and then get into the ground floor. There they placed explosives and destroyed the whole house.

This was a taste of what would come later in the campaign, as the battle for Manbij turned into an attritional slugging match. However, for now we continued to advance, though our logistics were disrupted and took a while to get back up to speed. This meant living off the few tins of food that we had stashed for such an event, and anything we could scavenge. Sometimes kind villagers would offer food, but they had their own issues. At the advancing front many civilians were reliant on foodstuffs provided by the SDF and the civilian authorities until the fighting had moved up far enough for normal markets to reopen, as enterprising souls, of whom Syria seems to have more than its fair share, would head off to cities in Rojava to buy provisions that they could sell on.

And here we are, back where this tale began. It was the lack of food that led me to that episode of sampling the delights of unripe pistachios where I began this story. We had been fighting for days and nights, piling into our ancient MTLBs and panzers and advancing against villages, and even individual houses if resistance was fierce, keeping up the advance to surround Manbij. But it was a grind, and from what we heard the other battle groups looking to complete the encirclement were seeing heavy fighting as well. I had watched an RPG team obliterate a Daesh fighter only a half hour before and now was sitting in the sun to catch a brief rest. The first Daesh mortar hadn't fazed me. The second, which followed twenty seconds later, meant it was time to find something a bit more solid to sit against as it looked like I was due a barrage. A bomb falling close to or on you would spell the end, but getting hit didn't really worry you. It was just one of those things.

I headed around the building, which would provide cover against anything but a direct hit. It was while I was resting here that some of my fellows brought me some unexpected bounty. First, one of the Kurdish snipers wandered up with a sack of peaches and gave me three. Fresh fruit! Things seemed to be looking up.

Then one of the Belgian volunteers came over. He'd found something that he wanted my opinion on. It was a notebook that had been written by a Daesh fighter in English. Given that he spelt 'colour' with a 'u', I suspected he was of British origin. But this wasn't why my comrade had sought me out. Inside were detailed notes from someone who had undertaken an advanced sniper class.

When people ask me about what I did in the war I generally answer 'I was a sniper', but this is just to simplify the conversation. I am under no illusions that my limited training comes anywhere close to the specialist instruction that a military sniper undergoes. This person, whoever they were, had received such an education. The notebook was full of meticulous notes that covered a range of factors and details affecting a shooter's performance. There were notes on the performance of different types of sniper rifle, how the particular calibres of bullet they used worked under different climatic conditions. There were lessons on the markings that different ammunition manufacturers placed on their wares and how the performance of those different brands of the same ammunition varied from one another in minute detail. There were lessons in how heat and altitude affected different bullets' trajectories, and notes on the average monthly temperatures in parts of northern Syria. There were also records taken from his experience of shooting, principally the correct settings – his clicks – for a particular scope and weapon that would allow him to shoot accurately to various distances.

It was, I will admit, troubling. Daesh had a reputation for fielding excellent snipers, with the Chechens in particular having a formidable reputation. But this was clear evidence of an extremely thorough and comprehensive training programme that had to have originated from an experienced trainer.

'Where did you get this?' I asked.

'It was on the road by two bodies that had been hit by an airstrike,' he replied. 'Does it mean anything to you?'

'Yes. Were there any weapons?'

'No. We thought they were civilians, but then I found this.'

They hadn't been civilians, that was for sure. Also in the notebook were sketches of the local terrain. And SDF positions and movements.

We continued to grind away at the enemy, and on 17 June a situation made me very aware of how the stubborn resistance and heavy casualties were affecting the mindset of some of the SDF troops. I was sent to support a tabor that was tasked with seizing a small town a few kilometres outside Manbij. We used an APC to launch a surprise assault in the early afternoon and captured a few houses to establish our perimeter. We'd met no resistance, but we did find mines in some of the gardens and strung from some trees, and the town was full of civilians who warned us that there was a strong Daesh presence dug into tunnels under us. Our commander realised that we had possibly got in over our heads and ordered us to occupy rooftops and prepare to defend ourselves. From our positions we could see little as it was quite well built-up and there were a lot of trees that obstructed our view, but my location on a higher roof gave me a good view of a road that ran along one side of the mosque dominating the area and would probably be one of the key routes of any Daesh counterattack. It was, quite frankly, a perfect target. The road ran straight as an arrow in front of me for a distance of between four and six hundred metres. It was a shooting gallery: anyone coming down it would be in my line of fire for the whole length. An assault would get a hard time from me alone before any additional fire was put into them. I was extremely pleased to have such a position; it was a dream shoot. My orders, however, were not so acceptable.

'Shoot anyone who comes down that road.'

Putting it down to my poor Kurdish, I assumed that I had misunderstood the soldier passing on this instruction.

'Yes, I will shoot any Daesh who comes down the road.'

'They're all Daesh here. No one comes down the road.'

In previous fighting, it had been plain that I was only to shoot if I saw a threat. My targets had to be armed or, like the unlamented suicide bomber of a few days past, present an obvious danger. I understood that we were in a very dangerous position with barely a toehold in the town and no support, so I assumed that I was expected to keep civilians off the road with warning shots.

I did not have to wait long before a man turned into the end of the road and started walking towards us. He was carrying a kettle and didn't seem to be at all concerned. While no doubt everyone now knew the SDF had taken part of the town, he was displaying the typical nonchalance that civilians in Syria always adopted in the face of armed troops – I'm no threat, I'm not a soldier, why shoot me?

'Civilian coming,' I told the SDF guys with me and settled for my shot.

My rifle hadn't been zeroed for some time and had taken a shaking in the APC ride, so I was worried about how my zero might have wandered. The Dragunov has excellent resilience against this, much better than more precise rifles which can lose a zero at a slight knock, but I wasn't about to risk a man's life. So I picked a spot on the edge of a mud house two metres to his left and a metre above his head. The bullet smacked into the exact aiming point I had sighted, which confirmed that both the rifle and I were on good form today. The man ducked and picked up his pace to a hurry but pressed on, evidently intent on getting the tea to its destination. It's possibly a dangerous assumption to make, but he struck me as exactly what he appeared and didn't present a threat.

'Why didn't you shoot him?'

'What?'

'You should shoot anyone who comes.'

'He's civilian.'

'No civilians here. All Daesh.'

I turned away from my scope and regarded the soldier. This was a very bad development. When soldiers start talking about entire populations as their enemy it is a recipe for massacre.

'No one comes down that road. Shoot to kill,' he said.

Fuck that, I thought. There was no way I was going to shoot someone in cold blood who presented no obvious threat. And I wasn't about to follow an order to murder civilians from some untrained little snot who had been born yesterday. Fortunately, I knew my shooting was spot on today and that gave me another option, which I was able to demonstrate a few minutes later.

Another man started strolling down the road. He was chatting amicably on a mobile phone and looked to be walking without a care in the world. If anything, his demeanour looked a bit too chilled, considering what was happening in his town, but though I thought him suspicious he didn't appear to be armed. This guy needed to get the message that the road was closed in no uncertain terms, so that he could spread it around to everyone.

I took careful aim and settled for the shot. I couldn't afford to mess this up, or else I'd be guilty of shooting a civilian.

The bullet struck the ground nine inches to the left of his foot, exactly where I'd aimed.

The ground was rock hard and there was some risk that the projectile would ricochet into him, but I was confident that it would bounce up the road. As it was, it performed just as I predicted, and though he would probably be picking splinters out of his legs he obviously suffered no serious injuries as his reaction was, I'm afraid to admit, somewhat comical. He went up into the air like a jack-in-the-box, his legs shooting out to either side, and then turned and raced back up the road at a rate most Olympians would have trouble matching.

This may sound like I am being cruel, inflicting terror on an – as far as I know – innocent person. But the alternative would have meant me being pulled off the position and the other sniper being put there instead. And he might well follow his orders.

I lifted my head and turned to look at the SDF soldier.

'Road closed. No one else will come,' I said.

And no one did.

Daesh were indeed aware of us and deeply entrenched in the town, as the next day would prove. We spent the night on watch with our thermal scopes and then, as the sun rose, Daesh suddenly peppered us with machine gun fire. I suspect it was just a probe to try to find where in the village we were, as there appeared to be only four men. Our return fire soon drove them off, except the machine-gunner, who overstretched his luck and went down hard.

The sudden appearance of an armed party only a few hundred metres from us raised further suspicion of what our intelligence had warned us of – that there was a tunnel structure in this area. Reports had it stretching all the way to Manbij itself, perhaps seven kilometres away. I can't say if this is accurate, but that Daesh had subterranean emplacements was certainly true.

As we watched through the day, one of the SDF pointed out a blue tarpaulin sheet that obscured the side of one house. He said that the sheet had shifted slightly and he was sure there was a tunnel or bunker entrance behind it, and that he had seen men. It was close to where our attackers had popped up, which made it worth studying. While we watched, more of the troopers insisted that, yes, they could see someone peeping around the sheet. This left me in a quandary. The other observers were using binoculars with much better magnification than my scope. But I also knew from long experience that the SDF tended to fall into a sort of group behaviour in these situations. If one claimed to have seen something, they all claimed they had seen it. If one claimed to have shot a Daesh, they all claimed to have shot a Daesh. And for the life of me I could not see what they claimed they were seeing. But their insistence that there was someone there, that he was twitching the sheet to look at us, got more and more vocal and insistent.

I stared and stared through my scope. And I couldn't see what they all said they could. I began to think that I had misunderstood, that my poor Kurdish had led me to look at the wrong area.

'The blue sheet? By the wall of the house by the road?'

'Yes, he is right there. Shoot!'

I couldn't see anyone. I was sure I was looking at what they were; there was nothing else that matched the description. I had taken up all the slack in the trigger and I was braced to shoot. But I didn't want to shoot at nothing.

A shadow flickered across the tarpaulin, cast from the other side.

I shot.

'You missed!' one of the Kurds cried.

And a wall of automatic fire hit our building. It seemed that every window and nook in the ground sprouted a muzzle flash. A furious gunfight erupted as the SDF started firing back. I could barely use my own gun as every time I fired, return shots peppered my loophole and drove me into deeper cover.

After an hour the firefight petered out, but the level of

resistance meant that command was worried about leaving us exposed, and with little hope of support. So, a few hours after nightfall, we silently retreated in good order across the fields to a farm outside of the town. We then set a large ambush and waited to see if any Daesh followed up. They did not and so we marched a few kilometres to a position in the rear where we could bed down. There I was to receive some news that restored my damaged reputation.

My partner sniper had tapped into the Daesh radio channels. It was a favourite trick of the SDF and the Arabic speakers would fill us in on what was being talked about – always useful. My partner rushed over to me with a look of glee on his face.

'Botan, Botan, let me tell you what they were saying.'

Daesh were on the radio. They had suffered one dead and two wounded, and were arranging a burial. They were cursing the Kurdish snipers, who seemed to have used supernatural abilities to kill their colleague. He had not been exposed; the cover to the tunnel had been in place when they shot him through it. The devil must guide their hands . . .

The next day was our turn to mourn. One of the snipers in our tabor had been killed. As a small, tight-knit group, it was a serious blow. Many of the infantry units had taken heavy casualties and we hadn't even reached the city. Morale was suffering and Daesh evidently were going to fight us all the way. We got an example of this when a sniper bullet passed overhead as we waited for orders at a command post. As the other fighters scattered for cover I raced up onto a rooftop to see if I could spot the shooter. I was soon joined by others who had the same idea. A British Special Forces sniper came up a minute later. He hesitated when he saw me, but I waved him up. This was a great opportunity.

'Set up, I'll watch for him. If I see him, you shoot him,' I said.

He, after all, had training and experience far superior to my own and his rifle was a precision-killing instrument with vastly better range and accuracy than my Dragunov. Two sets of eyes could cover more area and together we had a much better chance of getting the sniper than him getting us. He was happy with this and lay down behind his rifle and began scanning.

The British soldier's presence had been noted, however, by our own side, and we were joined by a mob of SDF with a machine gun, who came up and started shooting single shots – as was the SDF way of using a machine gun – at everything that may have concealed a sniper. I stopped looking and settled down into cover. I was unlikely to spot anyone out there and the machine gun would only draw attention. If a sniper looked us over he might well spot me and I would be the priority target. It may sound callous, but now the SDF were bait. If one of them got hit I should be able to tell from which direction the shot had come. There was no point in telling them to get down; they were set on finding the sniper and being heroes, hoping to impress the foreign soldier.

I also had to shoo interested SDF away from the sniper's equipment. Always suckers for a gizmo, they were fascinated by the plethora of technology that he had laid out around him and couldn't resist investigating. SDF troopers came wandering up to stare at the bonanza, many with hungry looks on their faces. Although theft is harshly punished by the SDF, it does occur, and the chance to acquire some sort of super-technology would likely be too much for some. The sniper was glued to his scope, so I had to act as guard dog and tell the hevals to leave well alone instead of actually trying to find whoever had shot at us. Meanwhile, the machine gun continued to shoot seemingly at random all over the place.

'Hey, mate. Do you know what they're shooting at?' asked the sniper.

The French in Al Hawl. The Americans at Shaddadi. The British at Manbij. Three for three. I still find this funny.

Eventually it became apparent that the Daesh sniper had cleared off. We settled down again, but in my case not for long. I was sent out to support a night mission by sabotage, who went well forward of our lines to mine a road that was being used during the day. After that I bedded down on the front to support a tabor that was holding our forward positions. As I've already pointed out, units could be very variable in their quality. I was made aware of how bad this unit was when I was promptly woken at six in the morning (bearing in mind that I had spent most of the night sneaking around in the dark) by the tabor commander blasting away with my Dragunov. Not content with wasting my ammunition, he took it upon himself to start messing around with the settings on my scope. Getting and maintaining an accurate zero is the most important aspect to using such a weapon effectively, and in one moment of utter stupidity this idiot had now removed my ability to do my job properly. And as he was the commander I couldn't even bawl him out. I realised that not only had he screwed up my zero, but this was the person who had been manning the machine gun on so-called counter-sniper duty the day before. I recognised that the unit was commanded by a complete idiot, something that was reinforced when, later that day, I was confronted by a furious German volunteer, who had been manning the most forward position.

'What the fuck? You nearly hit us, you arsehole!' he screamed in my face.

When I explained that it had been his own tabor commander who'd nearly killed him he wasn't in the slightest surprised. It was something that I had been hearing from every foreign volunteer: a deep dissatisfaction with how the SDF was conducting itself in this campaign. Many feared their own colleagues would get them killed through stupidity and bad tactics.

I had my own experience of this on the same day. Having decided to limit my exposure to the unit's ability to get me killed, I had set up an observation post in an old pigeon coop. This showed the love that Syrians feel for these birds, as it was the best constructed part of the building. The coop, located on a roof, had walls thicker than the rest of the house, being double breeze blocks with concrete poured into them. Three small ventilation holes provided useful loopholes in the thick walls, through which I could watch for Daesh movements. We knew that they were out there, but they were proving to be very adept at avoiding being spotted. The same, I'm afraid, could not be said of us.

I was ensconced in my ersatz bunker, scanning the houses that we suspected were Daesh positions. If I could pick out where they were it would make it considerably easier to advance against them when the time came. Nothing could be seen, but I was out of the sun and, though the interior was as hot as a sauna and stank of pigeons, I was happy to sit and watch. Unfortunately, the importance of not letting the enemy know where you are may have been understood by the Daesh forces we were facing here, but not by the members of this tabor. One of them came up onto the roof and ran over to see me.

'Botan, you good?' he asked.

'Yes, fine thanks.'

He then dashed back across the roof and down again. This activity must have drawn the attention of a Daesh watcher. To see a person dart out to a possible position and then run back the same way indicated all too clearly that someone was in there.

Knowing this, I stayed crouched down behind the thick walls and waited. I had been worried about a sniper trying a shot at one of the loopholes and so gave it some time to see what happened. Nothing. I had to assume he had been spotted, but after half a minute I thought it might be safe to take a peep. I rose up to edge one lens of my binoculars over the corner of one of the holes to have a look. I had been wrong and the time I had given had allowed not a sniper to set up to shoot at me, but a machine-gunner. As I slowly moved back into position he sighted in and opened fire.

The first round hit the wall at about chest height. The rest walked their way up to my loophole in less than half a second. Fortunately this provided enough warning and I had already dropped to the floor. There, lying in mounds of pigeon shit, I curled up and clamped my hands over my ears as rounds slammed into the coop or, worst of all, came through the hole and proceeded to ricochet wildly around inside. The noise was horrendous, like a jackhammer right by my head. It was, I'm sure you understand, unpleasant.

I have been asked what it is like to be in a position where you are liable to be killed at any instant. What are your thoughts when you are in a situation like this? I cannot speak for others, but I find that I become exceptionally focused. Watching bullets ricochet off the walls as another person tries to kill you should, I suppose, make you retreat in panic. That would be the logical thing to do. I don't react like that. Instead, I get extremely dispassionate about the situation, so that it becomes almost like a problem that needs solving. My position is revealed: what do I do about it? Where do I move to? Can I identify the enemy and neutralise him? Later, once the gunfire ended and I was able to slither away on my belly across the roof to get into better cover, would come fury. But there wasn't any point even raising the issue. The fool who had nearly got me killed wouldn't understand what he had done, and would be baffled by any complaints I might make.

Having had one lucky break, I asked to be allowed to move position as this one was known to Daesh. But this was refused; the snipers were to stay in the house and that was that. The foolishness of this, and that Daesh had us well marked out, was again demonstrated the next morning, 21 June, when as I rose out of my blankets in the early dawn light a sniper put a bullet past my head, missing by inches. The top of my head must have barely shown above the parapet but it was a reminder that one slip, no matter how slight, would kill you. Plenty of my SDF comrades, Kurds, Arabs and foreigners, would pay that price before this campaign was over. I had been lucky once again.

That opening shot was the start of another day of combat, and at 1100 a hell of a fight developed as both sides went at it. This was actually part of an overall plan and the SDF pulled off a textbook attack. While we pinned down the forces to our front, armoured personnel carriers deposited SDF infantry onto their flanks. Other parts of the village, including where we had retreated from a couple of nights before, suddenly had large numbers of our forces attack, and we rolled over the resistance by 1300. Daesh had been driven out, but they were still determined to fight us at every point.

The unit I was with moved up to houses next to some olive groves and forest on the edge of town. Here Daesh got bloody awkward. Their fighters used the cover beautifully, flitting between shelter and shadows and sniping at anything that moved on our side. We spent the afternoon fruitlessly trying to find them, all the time taking fire, but their skill was such that I never did spot anything solid. I scanned the surroundings for hours, every clump of grass becoming a man in a ghillie camouflage suit under my gaze. To shoot at a target that you weren't sure of was to give away your position and invite retaliation. It had developed into the ultimate high-stakes game, sniper against sniper, and the winner would be the one who walked away.

Still, despite all the fire exchanged it ended as a no-score draw. An SDF unit moved forward and took a house that stood a few hundred metres in front of us among the olive groves. This quietened Daesh down. I pulled four hours' watching through a thermal scope but nothing moved at all. It seemed that Daesh had had enough and withdrawn, probably to consider their options. That assumption was nearly to have severe consequences.

After my shift, and apparently unnoticed by the other sniper (who I'm sure slept on his watch), the forward position was abandoned. Command obviously caught wind of something or anticipated an attack and withdrew the infantry tabor holding the building. This was probably a good move as they were very exposed, but evidently a mistake was made as no one told us. Our position now unknowingly became the front line and we had just two snipers, a YPJ commander, her assistant and the commander of the anti-tank unit to defend it. Our location was even worse as the abandoned position stood higher than our building and overlooked our roof, where we were sleeping.

I first became aware that we might have a problem when someone made a spirited attempt to kill me with a burst of automatic fire while I slept. I was jerked awake by the sound of bullets hitting the concrete beside me and instinctively rolled away from the spurts of dust and debris that kicked up two feet from my face. If the shooter had been a little bit better and had fired single shot I probably wouldn't be writing this.

I grabbed both my rifles and scuttled across the roof bent so low that I was in danger of kneeing myself in the chin. The rest of our small party had also scrambled into the cover presented by the parapet walls or stairwell and were trying desperately to figure out just what the hell was going on. My first reaction was to get to a loophole and try to locate the enemy.

We were taking considerable fire from our old position, but I could also see movement in the olive grove. Daesh, having found one target clear, had evidently decided to rid themselves of us as well. Fighters in the house maintained continuous fire to keep us suppressed. At the same time an assault group was leapfrogging towards us, rushing forward in sprints and then dropping into cover while others covered them and added to the weight of fire against us. It was, I must admit, an impressive demonstration of proper infantry tactics.

I was using my Dragunov to pick off targets as they rushed forward, but every time I fired I had to duck back down as withering fire hit the wall around whichever loophole I'd used. The Daesh troops had got close to the edge of the grove and I didn't need to be told what would happen next. We'd be hit by everything they could throw at us – machine guns and RPGs especially – and then they'd rush us. They had to cover about one hundred metres of open ground and then they'd be at the building. There were two doors by which they could enter, and if they did get in we would be lost.

I laid down my rifle and switched to my Kalashnikov. I didn't really have much of a plan, but an idea had formed. As they rushed I would lay as much accurate fire into them as possible and then, just as they got to the house, I'd come out at them. It was a terrible plan, but the only option I could come up with was to hit them with as much aggression as possible and try to break their attack.

I thought we were all about to die.

And then the UK Special Forces soldiers walked a trail of 40mm grenades along the edge of the olive grove. I know it was them as I had seen them using that weapon on a target a few days earlier, and I knew they were still in the neighbourhood.

The Daesh troops milled around, screaming. The grenades had inflicted serious casualties on them and they were dragging bodies away. It might not seem fair, but I laid into them with my AK as fast as I could fire and reload. I had looked deep into the abyss. And someone had pulled me back.

I turned and ran back up the stairs to tell my comrades that we needed to get on the radio and have them aim fire at the house that had been providing the fire support. I had just reached the roof when the bombs fell about four hundred metres from us. As the first went off all I felt was the heat from the blast and instinctively I turned towards it. So I saw the second that was following it down. It was like it was falling through treacle, so slow did it seem to me. A long, white cylinder with bright green writing on it. It fell through the blossoming explosion and added to the fury. It was one of the most incredible things I've ever seen.

My awe was soon constrained by the zinging shrapnel that tore past me, and I threw myself flat on the roof as steel shards whistled overhead. The day had only just started and I had already used more than my fair share of luck. The strike had been on a Daesh emir, a senior commander, who had been in charge of both the defence of this outer perimeter around Manbij and commanding the attack on us. He had been too long on his radio and had paid the price for it.

Daesh evidently decided that enough was enough and cleared out. We slumped down, exhausted. We'd put up a ferocious defence but there was no doubt that we had come within a hair of disaster this morning. The commander was really not happy and, after a lot of snarling on the radio, an infantry unit was bussed up in an APC to replace us. I was grateful to be moving back to the rear, even if it was only a couple of kilometres or so, as I had well and truly had enough. And when I got back there was another bonus. The guys who had pulled my bacon out of the fire were hanging around waiting for their next mission. I got a chance to go and thank them, including the sniper I'd been with a few days before. He was pleased to tell me that he'd got the Daesh sniper we had been looking for the next day, at a range of seventeen hundred metres. And then for good measure they gave me a whole carton of their ration packs, a bounty I could only have dreamed of. Alas, the other foreign volunteers soon sniffed them out and I ended up handing most of it over to them. We were, after all, all in the same boat.

By the next day the SDF had got into the edge of Manbij, but here we started to find just how well Daesh had planned for our arrival. I had been pulled off the front for rest and was standing on a rooftop with Larry, the Swede who had joined the snipers a couple of months before. From three kilometres outside the city we watched a distant gun battle as a tabor moved in for a night attack to clear a district. But Daesh now revealed a new trick, or rather an enhancement on one of their old favourites. As the unit moved deeper into the houses the whole neighbourhood exploded in a titanic blast. Daesh had wired up more than a dozen buildings with a massive quantity of explosives and, once the tabor had been committed, blew the whole lot.

They also displayed how utterly ruthless they could be, and how they intended to use civilians as a shield against us. We had heard several accounts of fleeing civilians being mortared to force them to return to Daesh-held territory. On the 23rd a fresh atrocity occurred. A large number of men, women and children tried to flee to our lines through a Daesh minefield. These devices were command detonated: when they were sure they could do the most damage to make their point, Daesh exploded a large mine among the group. They killed six and injured eighteen that I heard of, many of them children. This brutality, and the heavy fighting we had endured just to reach the city, showed that Daesh had planned a defence in depth and intended to fight it out.

12

The Team Forms Up and Goes into Action

July 2016

Larry and I were in a quandary. Both of us had had very bad experiences supporting the infantry tabors, most of which had taken such levels of casualties that they were being pulled off the operation and sent back to Rojava to regain their strength. Morale had been hard hit and it was evident that the SDF's over-confidence in their own abilities and the success they had enjoyed in previous campaigns had made them unprepared for the consequences of an all-out brawl in a city. In truth, all of the volunteers engaged with combat units expressed the same fears; the general attitude you encountered was 'I don't mind dying, but this is suicide!'

Most foreigners started talking about forming their own units. Our feelings for the SDF tore us. We all had deep friendships with SDF members, and dreaded the thought of seeing them get injured or killed. But we could all see that they were not prepared for this battle – the continuous stream of bodies heading back into Rojava was testament to that. It was also apparent that Daesh were still managing to disrupt our supply lines. On many nights heavy fighting and AC-130s roaring their rage could be heard. Some nights we would be put on alert to pull back and assist in clearing the route, though I never had to. You'd usually get warned of such an order by an escalation of gunfire off in the distance towards the river, followed by a huge amount of bombing that would shake the ground kilometres away.

Our states of mind weren't helped by the obvious toll that the casualties were having on the SDF. A number of personnel had to be pulled out and replaced due to battle fatigue, including many of the snipers. The snipers were to suffer several incidents that really hit their morale in this period. We lost a team member, a highly respected squad leader who was earmarked for great things, killed by a car bomb on 29 June. We also lost one of our tabor vehicles and a substantial amount of equipment, including a Zagros rifle, when they got hit by an ambush. The car had been carrying many of our women snipers, and they barely escaped with their lives. As it was, the event led to many of them being withdrawn from the campaign as they were clearly suffering from shock. Also gone was one of our precious BMPs, in the same action, to an anti-tank missile.

Still the battle for Manbij raged and demands had to be met. We continued to go out and fight, but our confidence in the SDF had dissipated. Moe and Curly would only work together, and now Larry and I followed suit. Though many of the snipers were very good, some were a menace to be around and we didn't want to take unnecessary risks based on another's stupidity. We also began to lobby hard to be allowed to work as a four-man team, under Moe's direction. This would make us more effective, while giving us a better chance of actually living through this battle.

Two further events convinced me that, to have any chance of survival, working as a team was an imperative. Firstly, we received a new commander for our sniper tabor. Our previous commander had left just before the Manbij campaign had started and we had been without proper leadership since then. He had been a deeply respected and experienced leader and we had not been surprised when he suddenly left the unit for other assignments – no doubt he was heading for higher command, for which he was eminently suitable.

With big shoes to fill, it was always going to be a challenge for whoever replaced him. Unfortunately, the man we received was obviously not up to it. In fact, he represented exactly the sort of commander for whom I have no respect or time – a political animal who had achieved the position through his connections and spent his time hanging around the chain of command to make sure he was seen. He also had an issue with the foreigners in his unit, though whether this was from a complete inability to deal with other people's perspective or a product of his party training and the negative views of foreigners that this can impart, I couldn't determine in the brief time I had dealings with him. However, considering the poor opinion he quickly generated among the Kurdish old hands in the snipers, he was certainly a really bad manager of people. He also brought with him a couple of sycophants, who couldn't conceal their dislike for foreigners. Fair enough. I didn't bother to disguise my dislike of them.

The second was a chat I had with the British Special Forces team. The day after the Brexit vote, I had managed to get a sliver of signal on my mobile phone and found out about the result. Later that day I came across the Brits hanging around one of the command posts and stopped to shoot the breeze.

'So, we're out then.'

'What?'

Despite all their satellite communications and other technology no one had bothered to tell them that the most significant event in British history since the Falklands War had occurred. I suppose it wasn't considered important for their mission.

We stood around talking about the implications of leaving the European Union for a while, then the sniper took me aside.

'You hear the fighting last night? We got cut off for hours.'

'Christ! Yeah, heard the bombing. Unbelievable that the bastards can still launch attacks in the face of that.'

'Yeah. Listen: things might go tits up here. This lot' – he nodded over to the SDF command, who were huddled in a meeting – 'they might not be able to handle this. Intel has it that Daesh are really coming after us to cut us off. Between that and all the fuckers in there' – he nodded towards Manbij – 'we might be about to get fucked. Tell the other volunteers that if that happens they should try and get to us or the other SF teams. If the shit hits the fan we'll circle the wagons and bring the storm down on every fucker.'

One should always heed the advice of a highly trained and experienced Special Forces trooper. Meeting up with other volunteers, I passed on the message. Many, like Kemal, were looking at doing the same as us in the snipers, and one tabor commander agreed to field a squad of foreigners. Moe, Curly, Larry and I simply presented a fait accompli and said that we would only operate in the field as a four-man team.

On 30 June we finally got our chance to demonstrate what we could achieve. Because we were considered to be causing issues, due to our insistence on working together, we were sent out to support an allied SDF unit. They were holding a substantial section of the line, including the area where our colleague had been killed by the car bomb the day before. The unit was excellent, one of the best I had worked with in my time in Syria. But they and the other SDF units were in real trouble. We were holding a suburb of Manbij, with several hundred metres of open terrain between us and the main body of the city. It was a natural defensive line for both sides, but Daesh had achieved local superiority by using snipers and heavy weapons. In the previous three days three SDF had been killed in this section by snipers and another two by some sort of heavy weapon, probably a recoilless rifle.

It was an almost perfect set-up for us to show how a team such as ours could utterly disrupt a battle front and inflict serious material and moral damage on an enemy. As Daesh dominated the area, the SDF had to keep hidden and scuttle across any open spaces quickly or risk getting hit. We intended to change that situation.

We spent the morning surveying the battleground. It was plain that although there were civilians close to the front-line buildings, none seemed to be in the houses and blocks that directly faced us. Most of these had murder holes and observation points knocked into them and we carefully identified and logged each suspicious point and building. While Larry and I conducted this, Curly was preparing shooting positions. He masked the brick to be removed with a piece of net curtain and then carefully chiselled away the block until there was nothing there apart from the face of the brick acting as a fascia. This in turn would have the cement at the edge cut away. Then, being careful to keep his mask in place, he would quickly remove the face of the brick. No one watching would see the tell-talc black hole of a removed brick suddenly appear, a lethal giveaway. We would only expose the holes to shoot, and they would be covered by a sandbag as soon as we finished.

Having prepared our positions and identified likely targets, we got ready to announce our presence. Moe set up with the Zagros while Curly used his Sako. Larry spotted for Curly, I spotted for Moe.

'Go.'

We moved the covers and the two snipers started shooting. Because Curly's rifle was only a standard calibre he concentrated on suspicious windows and closer holes that he could put rounds clear through. With the Zagros Moe would aim not just at the murder holes but also below and to the sides of them. If any observer ducked back into cover he was liable to find himself hit by a round a few seconds later as the big bullets punched through the walls.

We comprehensively worked the ten most likely identified targets. Such a use of firepower was alien to the SDF and the tabor gathered to gawp as we basically tore a large section of the neighbourhood apart with accurate fire. And then the sandbags went straight back into place and we decamped to a back room away from any retaliatory fire.

Evidently we had upset someone, because suddenly a thick black oil fire started not far behind the Daesh front line. At first the suspicion was that perhaps one of our incendiary rounds had sparked something, but as the flames originated in a place where we hadn't shot it seemed unlikely. And then the penny dropped. The fire was one pre-set by Daesh to deter airstrikes. Our fire had riled up the enemy enough that they had lit one of their masking fires to try to stop us shooting.

Daesh might not like what we were doing, but the SDF commander absolutely loved it.

'That was great! How many did you kill? You must have killed many!'

We didn't know if we had hit even one. That wasn't the point, as we explained. The commander's radio was crackling with multiple requests from units all over the front to know what was happening. Impatient with the demands, the commander retuned his radio while we conducted our team debrief. We were happy with how it had gone and we had started planning our next moves when the commander whooped and interrupted us. He had found a Daesh frequency. They were screaming.

'They are trying to figure what happened to them. They have many casualties from the shots through the wall.'

One of the locations we had hit, which we had actually given special attention to as it looked so much like a position, had apparently housed a number of Daesh. As the shooting began they started to man their positions, only for Moe to put rounds through most of them. By the sound of it we had inflicted something of a toll.

Pleased with our success, we returned to the sniper rear position to sleep, but the next day were sent back to the same unit. The commander, a man with some political clout, had requested we return to him. As the new sniper tabor commander was put out by our refusal to play nice and deploy in pairs as he wanted, where he wanted, no doubt he was more than happy to get us out of his hair.

So 1 July started what would become an intense period of battle for us, though we weren't to know that. What we did know was that the Daesh snipers had gone quiet. That could mean they were cowering, but it was more likely that they were waiting for us to make a move so they could then try to take us out. To our great advantage was that we were operating as a four-man team, something the SDF did not do, and that gave us a lot of extra eyes and firepower.

We decided to repeat the tactic we had used: a sudden barrage on a range of different targets. After all, Daesh might have not taken the hint. We did this, and had retired downstairs to grab something to eat when a .50 calibre bullet came through the wall of the neighbouring room with an almighty crash and buried itself in a dividing wall. We dug it out and lined it up with the entry point. This gave us an idea of where it had originated.

We snuck back onto the roof and used our discreet view holes to look over likely positions for an enemy sniper. The gauntlet had been thrown down, but there was no honour in this duel. All we wanted to do was kill them.

We set up the Zagros and, the best options identified, laid into them. As Moe fired the rest of us watched his fall of shot and for muzzle flash from any return fire. I can't say for sure if we got our guy, but we did see two men run out of one of the target houses, jump on a motorbike and tear off into the city. As no fire came back we figured they were probably our problem pair and had wisely cleared off.

Daesh still weren't finished with us, though. Evidently piqued by whatever they were facing, they decided to have a good look. As we sat cleaning our weapons for the next shoot I heard the distinctive buzz that I had grown to recognise and loathe.

'Fucking drone!' I yelled and raced up the stairs with my Kalashnikov, closely followed by the others.

The SDF were alarmed by our actions, and even more so as we slid across the roof, turned over onto our backs and began to scan the sky.

'It is American,' the sentry called to us.

'Like fuck it is. It's Daesh.'

Drones are, by design, hard to spot. It is a matter of tracking by sound until you manage to lock onto it by sight. Even then, they can be extremely hard to keep in view as they tend to fade in and out of vision when at a distance. I don't know who spotted it first. I do know that once we saw it all four of us began to put a hell of a lot of fire after the damn thing. Certainly the radio once again started yelling questions about who was shooting so much and what was going on.

The Daesh pilot obviously realised that we were on to him and began to bob and weave to try to avoid our fire. But he wasn't daunted. Having turned away and climbed to a greater altitude he twice came back for another look. Each time, we were waiting for him. I was to curse long and hard about our lack of tracers, as all we could do was track the tiny shape in the sky and try to lead it with single shots in the hope of hitting something important, with no actual reference as to where our bullets were going.

But for all our fire, and that of neighbouring units who began to realise what we were after, I don't think we hit it, or at least not enough to down it. The drone turned and headed back to Manbij with desultory fire chasing it. And I suppose somewhere, on some Daesh computer hard drive, there's a video of four Westerners lying on their backs on a rooftop firing frantically up at the camera.

Our antagonist's persistence worried the SDF commander, and he suggested that we switch our position to keep Daesh off our scent, an eminently sensible idea. It was noticeable that since we had started operations here there hadn't been a single casualty among the SDF forces on this part of the front. We definitely had the enemy on the back foot and now we had to continue to maintain the pressure.

So the next morning we shot at the usual suspects and then shifted about a kilometre to our left into an olive grove. This had a small squad holding it and provided both plenty of cover for us to operate from and new views of our existing picked target, plus new buildings that were suspected of being Daesh positions. There was some concern from the SDF about us using the area, as the soldiers who had been killed by the recoilless rifle had been on watch here, but they had placed themselves in the only building in the grove, an old pump house, which was an obvious target. By staying down and using the trees and the low stone wall that surrounded the grove we could shoot from a multitude of places, which, along with our camouflage, would make it almost impossible for any Daesh watcher to get a bearing on us.

Once again we carefully logged all possible targets and planned to give Daesh a hell of a wake-up call the next morning. To maximise the impact all four of us would start shooting at first light; Moe with the Zagros, Curly on his Sako and Larry and me with our Dragunovs. We allocated specific areas for each of us. The theory was that this would really show Daesh that they had a serious issue on this stretch of front and that they could never be sure where we would strike from. They would be waking up to a firestorm, and they could either cower in their positions or try to fight. If they did the latter they would find themselves going toe to toe with a dedicated sniper squad.

As the early light broke on the morning of 3 July, we all opened fire simultaneously. For an hour we worked over various holes and windows, anything that Daesh might use as a fire or observation point. This may seem an extravagant use of ammunition, but in that time I probably expended only sixty rounds, mainly standard machine gun rounds that were adequate for hitting targets at these ranges, which went from three hundred to seven hundred metres. And the effort paid off.

As I shot at one murder hole a burst of return fire came from off to my left. Swinging my rifle round I scanned the house where I thought the shots had come from. Sure enough, a gentle drift of smoke was dissipating across its front, originating, I was sure, from one particular open window.

I watched for a few seconds, but could see nothing; the interior of the house was dark and I was staring into a black hole. I was sure that this was where the shot had come from. I could have waited (probably should have waited) but I had a target, the gun was on form and so was I. I thought about where I would be if I was in the target's position and lined up my shot, just above the bottom right corner as I viewed it. A right-handed shooter would probably be using that corner to maximise his cover. I squeezed my trigger, the rifle kicked, and I watched for an impact on the outside of the house to see if I had missed my shot. None came. My bullet had certainly passed through the open window, but being unable to see into the room I could not be sure where exactly. So I took up the pressure on my trigger again and waited. If a muzzle flash appeared I was ready to shoot instantly.

None came, and after two minutes of lying motionless I relaxed and resumed my previous fire pattern at the designated targets. I don't know if the Daesh had cleared off after his first burst, or if my shot had dissuaded him or hit him. But we took no more fire during the rest of the shoot.

Having made our presence well and truly known, we shifted back through the trees before sneaking a couple of hundred metres left into a neighbouring grove. At ten o'clock we shot again with the Zagros and Sako, hitting some of our favoured targets as well as some new ones that became apparent from the move.

Once again, we retreated into the trees and were enjoying a cup of tea with our SDF friends when suddenly mortars rained down on the position we had just shot from. It was nice to know that we had riled up Daesh enough for them to expose some of their heavy weapons to the attentions of the ever-circling coalition aircraft in an attempt to be rid of us. It was even better knowing that they were squandering their dwindling ammunition supplies as Manbij was now well and truly cut off by the SDF encirclement.

We figured that they had made their point and would leave it at that, so we started to relax. The grove was pleasant and shaded, and there was a water source running out of the ground via a hose pipe. We couldn't be observed and, though the area had been targeted by heavy weapons in the past, we were fairly well protected. In addition, the unit we were with was of good quality and their sentries were always on alert. It was a good place to spend the evening, and we decided to have another night and then go back to our original position to shoot the next day. That way Daesh would be kept guessing at where we were and we could keep up the pressure. Of course, the opposition also has a say in the game and they decided to make their own move.

We were sitting drinking chai and chatting when a shot rang out and the guard started yelling. And then the level of fire ratcheted up, the unmistakable sign that we were about to have an almighty fight. Daesh had somehow snuck a force forward to the houses just a hundred metres or so from our perimeter, which was the dry-stone wall around the grove. The SDF and our team rushed over to the wall and threw ourselves down behind it as the Daesh force started laying down fire.

'Right, we shoot in pairs. Five rounds rapid then drop and second pair shoots,' snapped Moe.

'Curly, Larry, you're first pair. Ready. GO!'

Curly and Larry rose, shot their flurry of rounds, dropped. Moe and I popped up from our cover and poured our own fire into the buildings. It's a suppressive technique to keep the enemy off balance and unable to respond effectively over the first half minute of the firefight. We burnt through our first magazines repeating this tactic. Daesh must have realised this wasn't going to be a walkover, and that they had run into a stronger force than expected as between us, and the SDF team with us, we were laying down a lot of fire, but they also weren't daunted and responded in kind. It was soon apparent that we were too strong for them to advance against, but also that we didn't have the firepower to drive them out of the buildings. The battle continued unabated as both sides sought an advantage.

I had just fired a volley of shots when a God-awful smell reached me. It was so rank I thought for a second that one of our guys had been hit in the bowels, or else we were being attacked with some sort of gas weapon. The stench was so strong it got pretty much our entire force's attention and we all turned to look, despite the fact we were engaged in a battle.

Curly was braced, his back against the wall with his trousers around his ankles, grinning at us madly. With bullets cracking overhead, he was passing one of the foulest-smelling things I have ever encountered. Even at a distance of ten metres it absolutely stank.

Moe, who'd been giving orders, stopped and gawped, his mouth slack with incredulity. Then his mouth snapped shut and in tones starting with disbelief and rapidly rising to rage he said:

'Are you kidding me, bro? ARE YOU FUCKING KIDDING ME??!!'

'What? I needed a shit,' said Curly.

It was too much for me. I slumped down against the stone wall and cried with laughter. Perhaps it was the adrenalin and stress of the situation, but it was just about the funniest thing I've ever seen.

Moe, however, had had enough.

'Right! Fuck this!' he said. 'Time to sort these bastards out!'

And with that he turned and, bent double, scuttled back into the grove.

'Where's he going?' asked Curly, who, having sorted out his toilet issue, was shooting at the enemy again.

'Fucked if I know.'

We soon got our answer. Moe came back on all fours, dragging the Zagros and ammo bag behind him. I couldn't help but laugh again.

'Knock, knock, motherfuckers.'

Moe got the rifle onto a tumbledown part of the wall that allowed him to sit behind the huge weapon. Not really having to aim much, he started smashing .50 calibre bullets into the target buildings as quickly as he could work the breech and reload. The Zagros was designed to punch through targets at well over a kilometre. At one hundred metres the impact of its API rounds, which I believe were originally intended to shoot down aircraft, really was something to see. Certainly Daesh got the point and we could hear panicked screaming from the houses as the huge bullets smashed through them. Using a heavy sniper rifle in a close-range firefight is not, needless to say, in any training manual I'm aware of, but the results were, without doubt, extremely effective. Daesh cleared out sharpish. We were very satisfied with the results of our handiwork.

The next day it was our turn to be on the receiving end.

We returned to our base position early the next morning, and the commander of the SDF unit wanted to explore a house further forward as he thought it might present a better shooting position. We had already looked it over and were concerned about its location. However, to keep him happy we agreed that Moe, Curly and I would go with him to look at it again while Larry stayed behind to provide overwatch with his Dragunov. It was apparent that our actions were gathering a lot of attention from the enemy, and so moving frequently to avoid getting hit by heavy weapons was a good idea.

Though the house was probably only a couple of hundred metres from our position, to get there entailed taking a dog-legged route as we passed through holes punched in walls and dashed across roads where we were exposed to enemy view. Carrying sniper rifles, AKs, body armour and all the other accoutrements of battle, we were heavily loaded and we gradually scurried our way to the house we wanted to explore. The only place to observe and/or shoot from was the first floor of the house, and to get there we would have to climb a set of stairs and sneak through a door that both faced the enemy. We lay on our bellies and wormed our way up, resisting the urge to move fast as this would catch any watchers' attention. There was a balcony on this floor, with a dense and ornate concrete balustrade that provided some cover, and we were able to crawl into the room we wanted to examine.

And it sucked. In addition to having to expose ourselves to simply reach the position, to watch or shoot from here would require making loopholes that, even if we disguised them, could well be spotted, especially after shooting something like the Zagros from them. Getting caught in this position under fire would mean that we would be trapped with our escape directly in the line of fire.

We had just explained this to the commander and were getting ready to move back out when one of his men came crashing in. I never did find out what he was doing; I assume he had some message he needed to convey. What he had done was reveal that someone was in the room to a Daesh sniper who was watching for an opportunity.

That first incoming round is always a shock, even if you are on alert. This was no different. There was an almighty bang, the whole room shook and Curly suddenly jumped to his feet with a roar and a spray of blood. The round, a .50 calibre, had come through the door and hit him in the calf. With hindsight, it must have clipped the balustrade, which absorbed a lot of its energy, as otherwise he probably would have had to have his leg amputated. As it was the effect was bad enough, with a great slew of muscle hanging down off his leg.

'Fucking cunt's shot me!' he yelled.

What seemed like a blizzard of fire hit the room and we all threw ourselves down. The whole building was vibrating as rounds struck it and seemed to physically lurch whenever another .50 calibre hit the building. Fortunately most impacted the balustrade but plenty more still tore through the breeze-block wall above our heads, showering us with debris.

We were in real trouble. Exiting through the door in

the face of this fire would be suicide, especially as we had a casualty with mobility issues. We couldn't see where the bullets were coming from, had no chance of returning fire and didn't even know if Daesh was closing on us. As the volume of incoming rose, it seemed likely that we faced an assault on our position. But we knew nothing for sure, other than that we were in serious trouble.

'Shit, I think they may be in the garden outside!' said Moe. 'Give me a grenade.'

I tossed him one of mine, an old Soviet model that probably dated back to the Second World War. He pulled the pin and, keeping low, lobbed it out the window.

Nothing happened.

'FUCK! FUCKING RUSSIAN SHIT! GIVE ME ANOTHER ONE.'

This time he got one of my German-made grenades. That did go off, with a satisfying thud. If Daesh were on the point of trying to charge us that would make them think twice, or at least we hoped so. In actual fact, what was happening was an almighty firefight as Larry, back in our home position with his Dragunov and supported by the rest of the SDF squad, engaged the enemy shooting at us. It goes to show how cut off you are from your surroundings in such a situation: we didn't know that anyone else was fighting. As far as we could tell we were taking a hell of a lot of fire and no one was doing anything about it.

Curly had dumped himself down and started dealing with his wound. You know you're with the right people when they can stay completely rational in the face of such damage, and Curly was probably the calmest of us all in that room. He finished applying the combat dressing, gave himself a shot of painkillers and hooked himself up to a bag of saline.

'Need to figure a way out of here,' he said, cool as the proverbial cucumber.

And that presented a problem. The floor was poured concrete and the back wall, leading away from the enemy, was very thick. In addition, we were on the second floor and would need a way to get down. The only option seemed to be the side wall, which faced the stairwell. The wall was only a couple of breeze blocks thick and punching through it would allow us to crawl out onto the balcony before rushing down the stairs to the garden.

The SDF guy produced a club hammer and set about smashing a hole. Being in such a situation gives one a tremendous impetus and he had soon knocked through. As he set about widening it so that we could fit through, the rest of us got our gear together so we could shift quickly. Getting to the top of the stairs, maybe just over three metres from us, would mean getting through a hail of fire. We would then have to get down the stairs in full view of the enemy with a wounded man. Still, as the old saying goes, it could always be worse. And it became so.

The SDF soldier had almost finished making the hole big enough. Unfortunately the clouds of white dust that his energetic tunnelling had thrown up had given the sniper team the perfect indication of his position. With an almighty bang a round came through the wall and struck him in the face, putting him down with a strangled scream and spraying blood across the room. Moe was on him in an instant, assessing and treating the wound. Now we had two casualties.

Again, it seems likely that the huge bullet had managed to pass through the thick balustrade plus the block wall before hitting the unfortunate victim; it may even have ricocheted off another wall. To get shot in the face with a bullet like that and not have your head taken clean off meant the round had used up considerable amounts of energy before it struck him.

I was to get a mild impression of the power of these rounds a few seconds later. Realising that Curly's Sako rifle was on the side of the room from which the fire was coming and could get damaged, I scrambled across and reached over to grab it from where it was leaning on the wall. Which exploded in my face.

I can only describe it as what being kicked by a horse must be like. I was knocked from my knees to the ground with a yell. I knew what must have happened. I had been hit.

My arm was screaming and with a sick feeling in my stomach I desperately felt for the damage. I expected to feel a hot slick of blood pouring from my arm but I could find nothing except a heavy coating of concrete dust that seemed to be covering my left side. Moe, still trying to stop the SDF trooper's bleeding, turned to me and said:

'You hit?'

'No. No, it missed me!'

The huge .50 calibre bullet had blasted through the wall and just missed me. However, the sheer energy of the round as it passed my arm had been enough to knock me to the ground. The next day a welt would come up on my arm that looked like someone had hit it hard enough to have broken a broomstick on it, and it would ache for several weeks. But once again I had been lucky.

A fresh storm of fire started sleeting past our supposed escape route, indicating that Daesh knew our plan, while barrages of .50 calibre slammed into our building, sometimes tearing straight through. Things were going south fast. The SDF soldier was coughing blood all over the place and groaning, Curly was sitting phlegmatically with blood seeping through his dressing, and the rest of us were pinned down.

'Botan, cover the stairs. If anyone comes up them, slot 'em,' barked Moe.

I took up the downed soldier's M16 and covered the top of the stairs through the hole that was supposed to be our exit. It was only ten feet away, but a continuous stream of small-arms fire was buzzing across the route. I lay prone inside the hole and focused on the top of the staircase. The first person who appeared over the edge of that top step was going to take a bullet in the face, which would be followed swiftly by a grenade.

The commander was on his radio, trying to get support.

'They have a ladder, but we have to get through the back wall,' he said.

'Right, fuck this!' said Moe and, taking up the hammer, began attacking the thick back wall in a fury. Quite amazingly, he started making an impression on the block and concrete construction, but it was slow going. With a roar he stood up and started slamming the sole of his boot into the wall. I was about to tell him to stop wasting his effort when he actually kicked a large hole straight through! I was astonished, and it just goes to show what can be achieved when you have the right stimulus.

In no time at all he had kicked a hole big enough for us to get through. Outside, SDF troops were waiting with a ladder.

'B, keep us covered while we get the wounded out.'

'Yeah, no worries.'

The guys managed to get down the ladder and I soon followed them. Daesh continued to pepper the building, but once we were down on the ground we were covered. We knew that Daesh might try to mortar us, so we had to pull back quickly. The SDF had punched new holes through the garden walls to minimise our exposure to enemy fire on the way back. Two of them tried to take Curly's weapon and equipment.

'Fuck right off, I carry my own gear,' he growled, and limped all the way back to base. I have to give the old bastard his due, as watching him walk out of there with his armour, gun and equipment, with that leg wound, was the most extreme demonstration of endurance I've ever seen. He's possibly the toughest person I've ever met.

The two casualties were loaded onto a pick-up and dispatched to hospital. We were depressed and angry. We'd been caught out and hit hard, but all in all we had been lucky – it could have been far worse. Now we were back at our primary position and we had our Zagros in hand again.

The sniper team that had pinned us down had pulled out and we started looking for Daesh to engage. We wanted – needed – to strike back as soon as possible, and searched for a solid target to hit. Daesh needed to know we were still in the game and that they weren't in control of the area.

The night before, the SDF had advanced on the hill to our

right and had been sporadically engaging in a close-range gun battle with Daesh forces in a house one hundred metres away. It was a far foray for us, almost a kilometre and a half, and we had to observe carefully to make sure we didn't engage friendly forces by accident. After watching for a while Larry called out that he had seen Daesh fighters moving on the rooftop of the building. As dusk approached Moe set up the heavy rifle while Larry spotted through binoculars. I watched the main front, our usual target area. It was possible that as soon as we fired we would attract attention.

'Set,' said Moe. 'Let's give it to these fuckers.'

The first two shots ranged in on the target and then Larry shouted out that he'd seen a hit on the parapet of the target building. Moe, now having the range and windage, began to blast rounds into the building as fast as he could load them. I have already spoken about the 'one shot, one kill' legend. With the right equipment that can be the case, but it is only part of what snipers do and there are other roles to play, especially with a heavy-calibre rifle. Here Moe demonstrated how one could be used as a wrecking ball.

'I can see them! You've got them pinned behind the parapet!' shouted Larry, followed by 'HIT!'

Our defiance would lead to a battle of wills between us and the enemy. The next day we again hit several murder holes and houses that we had shot before. This repetition was a way of making it plain that anyone wanting to use them for observing us or shooting would know we had the position marked and targeted. In this way we would continue to dominate our section of front. However, Daesh were not going to let us have it all our own way, and a sniper started shooting at me while I pulled guard duty. Fortunately the unit we were with had fortified the parapet wall with sandbags. As a result, if you stayed below the edge of the parapet you were reasonably safe, though having bullets smack around the observation points whenever you tried to sneak a look was disconcerting.

It was plain that our presence had started a lethal tennis match. We engaged, they engaged, and Daesh routinely mortared the area as well. We needed to up the ante to really establish dominance. This would prove invaluable if our infantry ever had to attack to get into the city proper. It also meant we were tying down units that might otherwise redeploy to fight in other parts of the city. Fortunately a couple of developments allowed us to really inflict some damage.

About nine hundred metres from us was a large building under construction. The foundations and part of the ground floor had been completed and, as it was slightly obstructed from our view by other buildings, we had paid it little attention. But now we noticed that a large tarpaulin had been stretched taut across one of openings that would probably have been a loading bay if the building had ever been finished. This caught our attention. The wind in northern Syria is quite strong. Such a large sheet of material would soon be blown to shreds unless it was maintained. It would also be perfect for hiding a defensive position or heavy weapon, which would have a great field of fire against anyone trying to advance across the open ground between the SDF and the heart of the city.

We settled down to watch, and soon noticed a couple of things. In one of the more open parts of the building, among the support pillars, someone had hung clothing to dry: men's shirts and trousers, all black – Daesh's colour. We were pretty sure we were on to something, and then we spotted something else. At the bottom corner of the big tarpaulin, a hand was very slowly pushing spoil out from under the cover. We had a new priority target.

A speculative shot with the Zagros convinced us that we were dealing with a major enemy position. A number of the heavy rounds hit the tarpaulin and detonated with sparks as soon as they penetrated. The tarp billowed in the wind and we figured that next morning we would be able to see what we had shot at as the cover was bound to have torn loose in the night. However, the morning revealed that the tarp had been repaired in the night and was back to its original tautness. Daesh might as well have put up a flag.

We needed more firepower and requested an airstrike, which would flatten the target in one go. But that was denied and we asked if there was anything heavier that the SDF could hit the building with. We had expected dushkas. What we got was much more satisfying.

We had just completed an observation watch when the commander of the unit we were supporting called us down to see the SDF's latest invention. I laughed hysterically when I saw it.

'It's a baby Şer!' I exclaimed.

'It's a Şer Portative,' the commander told me. 'We have been given it for testing.'

I had seen the Şer 14.5mm heavy rifles at the sniper tabor before they had been withdrawn from service. This new weapon had the unmistakable thick barrel of the Şer, but was much shorter, capable of being carried and used by one man if necessary. The Russian 12.7mm round is a powerful projectile, but the 14.5mm really raised the stakes. What we had was a one-man cannon!

The original Şer was a brute that needed two men to carry it and was meant to kick pretty hard. They also tended to destroy the scopes in about twenty shots or so. If such a beast could be a handful, how would this sawn-off version compare? There was only one way to find out, and we had the perfect target.

There was more good news.

'A mortar will come later. Moe knows how to use it, yes?'

All in all, Daesh had a very bad day. In the morning we shot the tarp and the unfinished building with the Şer Portative with satisfactory results. Though we again failed to get the tarp to collapse we could see the big rounds exploding inside the building with a great flash. The increase in firepower over the Zagros was marked, but not without cost. Our cheap Chinese scopes would suffer broken prisms almost immediately when used on the shortened version. Moe had to use all of his considerable skill and experience to fire with accuracy, having to adjust constantly as the crosshairs bounced and actually spun in the sight.

The new weapon also had some reliability problems. Unless the gun was kept meticulously clean and the huge rounds were well oiled as they went into the breech, they had the tendency to jam solid after firing. This would then require breaking down the gun and knocking out the casing by dropping the whole thing barrel-first onto a piece of protruding rebar on a nearby rooftop. It was not a particularly useful thing to be doing when you wanted to put rounds into targets, and we soon learnt that to use the weapon effectively required three people. Moe would shoot and snap open the bolt action, Larry would have greased each round ready and then loaded the weapon. I would spot the fall of shot and call instructions. In this way we could put rapid and heavy fire into target areas, which could be superbly destructive.

But, of course, this was just the start of the punishment we were going to hand out that day. In the late afternoon an 82mm mortar turned up. The weapon commander knew us and had respect for Moe's ability. The mortar got set up behind our house, the range and direction being worked from a tablet with a mapping program. To control the fire, Larry would watch the fall of shot from the front of the rooftop, where he would shout it to me at the back. I would then call down corrections to Moe, who was manning the weapon with the support of the Kurdish crew, with the exception of the commander, who stayed with us on the roof so he could enjoy the fireworks.

Dusk was setting in when we actually opened fire. The first bomb fell in line with the target, but about two hundred metres past it. The mortar commander was very happy with that. In his book that counted as a hit. He was somewhat surprised when Larry and I shouted out the fire corrections. The next bomb landed just in front of the target. The commander was overjoyed! These were excellent results. The third bomb whistled in.

'Hit! He landed it right on the target,' shouted Larry.

I turned and shouted down to Moe:

'Direct hit. FIRE FOR EFFECT!'

Moe didn't need telling twice, and started throwing bombs down the tube as quickly as they would fire. This was proper mortar work. Unfortunately the YPG crew were not used to such a rate and as the fifth bomb in the series, the eighth overall, launched they physically threw themselves on to Moe to stop him shooting any more. Our limited logistics once again thwarted us, and Moe had already fired more bombs than had been allocated to the fire mission.

Up on the roof we were oblivious to the row that had erupted and were enjoying watching the barrage hammer the unfinished building. A flurry of bombs rapidly burst in and around the structure, and it was gratifying to imagine the results on any Daesh inside. Then the fire ended, leaving us disappointed that more damage couldn't be dished out, but that was the way it was and we had certainly sent a clear message that this part of the front was going to cost them severely. They seemed to get the message, as the next morning a careful observation of the building showed no sign of activity and the clothing that we had seen had vanished.

Things went quiet for a few days. We periodically harassed suspected positions with sniper fire. I gave up my Dragunov for Curly's Sako rifle. I wasn't anywhere near as expert with it as he was, but by zeroing it at five hundred metres I could judge the fall of shot at different ranges with a reasonable level of accuracy. The Sako was a true sniper's rifle and firing it was a joy. The recoil was so slight as to be unnoticeable and the trigger so light that it required barely a touch to fire. It was an utterly different beast from the Dragunov and it was a revelation to be able to shoot a round and not have the cross-hair move off the target in the slightest.

However, this fight was not yet done. On 10 July Daesh struck back by shooting a 23mm gun from among the buildings in the city proper, which set a building behind us on fire, and then they bracketed our building with two mortar shells. We had overstayed in a single position and resolved this by moving out the next morning and returning to the olive grove. We chose some new targets well into the centre of town, perhaps two and a half kilometres away, that had caught our attention because of the amount of comings and goings; no doubt Daesh thought they were beyond any scrutiny in such a built-up part of the city. But a few shots from the Şer and the hammer blow its rounds made had men spilling out in a swarm and running off into alleyways or disappearing at high speed on motorcycles. Evidently we had upset some sort of meeting place or headquarters.

Unfortunately, the Şer was displaying signs of distress. We mothered it as best we could but, despite the cleaning and the oiling, the gun kept getting jams and had also developed an alarming tendency to blow flames out of its breech when fired. This gradually worsened to blowing the breech open on firing. With such a powerful round Moe was becoming worried about a catastrophic failure that could result in the weapon exploding beside his head. As a result we decided to minimise use of the Şer and switch back to the trusted Zagros.

To keep Daesh guessing we bounced back to our original position a day later and began to observe a building that the SDF sentries reported seeing suspicious activity around. As we watched the house in question, it was apparent that multiple men were coming and going. At a kilometre, this was a perfect range for the Zagros, so Moe put a round into it. Then we got a taste of what Daesh were going to implement as their standard tactic. I was acting as spotter and so was first to see it.

'Christ! Hold your fire! They've pushed a kid out in front of you!'

Through my binoculars I saw an armed Daesh drag a child around to the side of the building facing us, where the dust from the impact of our first round was still puffing in the air. He pushed the boy in front of the wall and then rushed back into cover. The boy looked over towards where the man had gone and then, obviously ordered to do so, started to hesitantly jump up and down directly between us and the target. The Zagros might be an accurate weapon, but there was no way we could risk shooting with a child so close to the line of the shot.

This pattern followed for the next few days. We would try to identify possible observation points where Daesh sentries were, or significant buildings, and engage them. This was pure harassment to keep the local forces off balance as much as possible. As Daesh realised we were going to be a problem they moved their obvious forces back into the centre of the city, but even out to almost three kilometres we were capable of hitting the larger buildings they were using with our heavy 14.5mm rounds. Alas, the Şer's extractor finally gave up the ghost and we were contemplating what we might do about this when we were recalled for a break.

We had been heavily engaged at the front for almost three weeks, so a rest was most welcome. But that did not happen, as we had to stand to. In the distance the bombing had once again ramped up and we were told that a heavy attack by Daesh was happening on the perimeter. We had to be aware of possible breakout attacks and so ended up keeping watch for part of the night. Because we didn't want to get caught out, the three of us decided to sleep downstairs on the rocky ground rather than get stuck on the rooftop that only had one staircase and about fifteen other SDF sleeping up there. We settled down, wearing our body armour and webbing, our weapons by our hands and with helmets as pillows, and fell into exhausted sleep.

A couple of useful developments had taken place while we were having our rest. The sniper tabor had been issued its own Şer Portative and this was handed over to Moe as he had the most experience on the rifle. We were issued with new ammunition, which we looked forward to testing as well. Up until then all we'd had were armour-piercing incendiary rounds which, while perfectly satisfactory, had less explosive or penetrative impact than dedicated rounds. With this new rifle we were issued with dedicated high-explosive and armour-piercing bullets.

We headed back to the same unit and decided to test the munitions on the unfinished building that we had mortared. It had been a few days since it had received any attention and it was apparent someone had repaired the tarpaulin, a sure sign it wasn't there by chance after the amount of fire we had directed at it.

The new Şer Portative performed perfectly and we realised that the first model must have had some manufacturing defects. The new bullets also proved to be a boon. The armour-piercing rounds would punch clean through the thick concrete walls and supports – I could see the splinters and dust showers that each threw up in the rooms we were targeting – but the high explosive really escalated our impact. Though the tarp obscured most of the entrance we could see into the top of the loading bay. The flash of the explosive rounds when they impacted was very large, like a grenade going off. Anyone sheltering in there would be having a really bad time. The fact that the tarp covered something solid, like a sandbag barricade, was made clear whenever a round hit lower down. It would detonate with a huge flash and bang, and the tarp sagged as it took damage.

This told us that there was, almost certainly, a Daesh defensive position in the building. And the opposition didn't appreciate our attention. We completed our shoot and headed downstairs into cover just as two mortars whistled down and landed around our house. The continued failure by Daesh to hit us with these weapons revealed the wisdom of the SDF commander in choosing this position. Our rooftop allowed both his sentries and us snipers to see a huge section of the city, but the buildings around us obscured the enemy's view of us and meant they couldn't see the fall of their ordnance to correct it.

Of course, mortars were not Daesh's only weapon and the next morning (18 July) we got a lesson in how much they wanted to have a crack at us. As we sat at breakfast a sudden explosion rocked our house, bringing dust down from the ceiling. We rushed upstairs to find the girl who had been on guard scrambling frantically across the roof to get into cover. A rocket had hit the balustrade right beside her and, understandably, she was in shock. We all thought it remarkable that the projectile hadn't landed on the open rooftop, which would have killed her outright, until we received a report from a sentry at another location who reported that the projectile had come from a window and streaked along in a straight line to our house. This hadn't been a Katyusha artillery rocket. It had been an anti-tank guided missile.

We set up and examined the house minutely. It was now that our careful hours of studying the terrain paid off. The window in question had a curtain pulled across it, but on other days we had seen through it clearly. Previous observations had noted that the side of the room facing away from us appeared to be broken down, offering a view through. This made it the perfect place to launch a missile from. Most anti-tank missiles produce a huge back blast – firing one in a closed room would likely kill the shooter – but with the rear wall down the blast would be directed into the open air. We had found our enemy.

It was possible that the missile crew had left the room straight after shooting; if they were smart that's what they would do. But we decided to shoot because such a weapon is heavy and cumbersome, and it and its crew might very well still be in the room. A response would also let Daesh know we were on to them and dissuade them from using the same room again.

The Baby Şer was the ideal weapon for this job. Moe started with the explosive rounds, putting the first two into the wall around the curtain. This tore it clear and allowed him to put three more into the room itself, where they detonated thunderously on the floor. He then followed up with AP rounds, which ripped through the walls like paper. Moe placed them all low and marched the fire up and down just above where we estimated the floor would be. If there was anyone in there and either lying on the floor or injured, that day was likely their last.

We received no more missile fire, so one way or another we had been successful: the missile team was either out of action or had decided it wise for them to stay away. But the next day we started taking sporadic sniper fire. Lone shots would ring out fairly regularly, but not at any particular target. Certainly no one reported getting hit, and confused radio messages from other SDF units crowded the airwaves as everyone tried to figure out who was getting shot at.

'This is for us,' I reasoned. 'They are trying to get us to shoot.'

The three of us were on the roof, scanning for the mysterious shooter. I was fixed on the unfinished building. The basement level was partially exposed. It showed nothing but impenetrable darkness, like a cave. Anyone under there could see out perfectly, yet be invisible to observers.

'If I were them,' I said to Moe and Larry, 'I'd have a sniper under there, all set and watching. They know where we normally shoot from now. They set this guy up to take pot shots to draw us out and try and nail us.'

'Yeah, reckon you might be right,' agreed Moe.

So, what do you do when you suspect a trap? Well, you don't trigger it, that's for sure. Besides, we had a request to shoot at a specific target that was suspected of being the entrance to a tunnel system. So we decamped once again to the olive grove, to engage the suspicious building.

Moe and I snuck through the trees so as not to give away our position. Our destination was a place where part of the stone wall had fallen down, giving us a view of our targets. Suspicious activity had been reported at a series of houses, with one small mud house being of particular interest. Sentries at several of our positions had seen people appearing and watching, but no one actually coming or going from the place. As there was no water supply evident, an absolute necessity in the summer heat, it seemed logical that the occupants must be moving to and fro to get supplies, hence the thinking that it housed a tunnel into Manbij. We were facing the front of the house, and we decided that if we could put some rounds through the door that should discourage Daesh from using it in the future.

We set up, Moe shooting and me spotting, and put four rounds into the first three houses that had been flagged up. The final one was the 'tunnel' house. The first two 14.5mm high-explosive rounds caused considerable damage to the exterior, blowing great lumps out of the wall. But the third really was the charm. It punched through the sheet metal door and then exploded. The effect was glorious. The whole door frame blew clean out and crashed to the ground. Moe and I shouted in celebration and he put another round through the gaping door frame, into the building. Then he heaved up the big rifle and retreated back through the grove while I covered him with my AK. Once he was clear I turned and ran back into the trees to avoid any return fire.

'Christ, bro! See that fucking door come off?' Moe laughed at me once we were back with our SDF hosts.

'Yeah, mate. No one's going to be using any tunnel there now.'

My good mood only lasted until the next day, unfortunately. Staying at the grove for the night, we were woken before first light to be told that one of the sentries had seen people moving and that we needed to get to the perimeter wall in case we were about to be attacked.

I had taken the far left position when one of the SDF hurried over to me. In the early morning half-light he had seen people heading for the Asayish position about a kilometre off to our left. I needed to engage them. I lifted my rifle and studied the group, who were flitting through the shadowy light and hard to spot. Even so, after a minute of watching them I was happy to conclude that they were a family fleeing the city for our lines. The man, woman and two small children, laden down with items, were hurrying as fast as they could to the Asayish point. It was logical that they would try to make their escape early in the morning as Daesh had, as already pointed out, been in the habit of killing those trying to run from the besieged city.

'It's OK. It's a family with children.'

The SDF trooper was adamant.

'They may be bombers. You should shoot.'

I turned away from my scope and looked at him.

'Maybe,' I replied. 'But I see no weapons or threat. Radio the Asayish and warn them that they have civilians coming. They know what to do to check them.'

'You must shoot,' he insisted.

'I don't have to do anything. They are not a threat.'

He spat in anger and then raised his own weapon. It was a silly move as the range was at least five hundred metres, way beyond any hope of accuracy with a Kalashnikov, and the light made any shot even more unlikely to be accurate. He should also have paid more attention to my tone.

The Dragunov is good at what it does, but in many ways it is a crude weapon. The safety is a good example of this. Mounted on the right side of the gun is a stiff lever that comes off with a loud 'clack'.

The SDF trooper froze when he heard that distinctive noise and turned his head. His eyes widened when he saw the barrel of my rifle pointed straight at him. He positively shrank when he looked me in the eye.

'No shooting. Radio the Asayish and tell them civilians are coming.'

This set a final doubt in my mind. I had deep reservations about what would happen when we had to fight in a city with a large civilian population. We all did. They weren't helped when we headed back to the rest area and ran into the French Special Forces guys. One of them invited Larry to come and watch as they conducted a reconnaissance with the thermal cameras mounted on their drones. The cameras showed all too clearly the conundrum that we would face. A Daesh fighter sat on top of a house, making a point of being visible to aerial view. The thermals showed that families still lived in the house below. Bombing was out of the question – it would kill all civilians in the house as well as the Daesh. An infantry attack would have to fight in among panicking civilians to get the Daesh hiding within them.

I wasn't willing to do that. Then news reached me that Kemal had been attacked by some men in his own tabor. They had been beating a civilian and he had intervened, and they had turned on him. For me it was the final straw, and when Moe pressed a SDF commander about what had happened to Kemal and what had been done to his attackers he was warned that if he didn't leave it alone he would be shipped back to a base in Rojava. What with the issues we were having with our commanders, our doubts about the abilities of the SDF and the concerns we had about being involved in a possible massacre of civilians when the final attack on the city began, this was the final straw for us all.

We quit.

13

Heading Home . . . and Getting Arrested

August 2016

We passed back through Sari Kani on our way out and picked up Curly, who was recuperating in hospital. It was great to see him, and he took great delight in rattling the remnants of the huge bullet that had hit him around in its clear plastic bottle. We planned to remain until he was fit to travel, but the tough old soldier refused to stay that long. We had been told that the only way out was several hours of walking, but Curly wasn't concerned.

While at the hospital we also got to see the SDF trooper who had been hit in the face when we were pinned down in that room. He also had a souvenir in the shape of the deformed .50 calibre bullet that the surgeon had plucked from his jaw, which had been, understandably, comprehensively smashed and had required bone grafts to repair it. But looking at the hunk of lead and steel that had hit him in the face it was remarkable that he was up and about and recovering well with his comrades in his unit.

After this we were sent on to Karatchok and began the standard wait to get out. There was a batch of fresh recruits there, undergoing the YPG's training for foreign volunteers. This had improved greatly since I had undergone it more than a year earlier; it now lasted a month, with a heavy emphasis on Kurdish-language lessons – a real boon for the new volunteers. Many of them were from political organisations, or else were young guys wanting to help. I'd noticed that the YPG had largely stopped taking on military veterans – I guess they got fed up with the lectures. The new volunteers naturally wanted to know all about the situation, what they would face out there, just as we had when we had come in the first time. I can't say we left them in good spirits. We told them that Manbij was going to be murder.

And murder it was. While I was waiting at Karatchok I heard that Gîvara the British farmer, whose real name was Dean Carl Evans, and Rodî – Martin Gruden from Slovakia – had been killed fighting in Manbij. More would follow. On 3 August Jordan MacTaggart from Colorado was killed. I had come in with him when I returned in January and we had met up many times since, including while fighting in Shaddadi. On the 10th it was the turn of Bill Savage. Bill, also from the United States, was a fighter who I had great respect for, solid in even the most adverse circumstance.

The fighting in Manbij would roll on until 12 August, when Daesh abandoned the city. I was back in the UK by then, but heard from those who had been there that they had been allowed to leave with hostages. Enough blood had been split for Manbij.

Our own exits were far from smooth. Curly and Moe left the day before Larry and me. We had expected to go to Sulaymaniyah to leave, but because the KDP was actively hunting for YPG foreign volunteers now and were checking vehicles on the road we found ourselves diverted to Erbil, where we received news that Moe and Curly had been picked up at a checkpoint and were in prison. Just because we were away from the combat didn't mean the threat was over, and it was with great relief Larry and I finally arrived in Sulaymaniyah, from where we could fly home. Moe and Curly, however, would spend more than a month in a KDP jail before being able to leave Syria.

On 1 August I arrived back in the UK, and was expecting the reception I got. As we disembarked, everyone's passport was being inspected.

Here we go, I thought to myself. Policy had caught up with the situation and it had become standard for British YPG volunteers to be arrested when we returned. Which is exactly what happened. The greeting party was from SO15, the Metropolitan Police's anti-terror unit. They politely told me that I was under arrest under the Terrorism Act 2006 for preparation of terrorist acts and training for terrorism, and I was taken away for questioning and finger- (and foot!) printing.

It was, to be utterly frank, all I could do not to laugh. Though these were serious accusations, with the potential for life imprisonment – as my lawyer worriedly told me – I wasn't at all concerned. I suppose that was due to two things. Firstly, I had literally dodged death so many times in the past month alone, let alone in the last year, that it was hard to take such a punishment seriously, ridiculous as that may sound. Secondly, I knew that even if a case could be brought to court, did anyone seriously believe that any jury in the land would ever find me guilty? Daesh cells and sympathisers were murdering people on the streets of European cities; our forces were actively engaged in fighting them. And here we have someone who went out to Syria, fought these people who are portrayed – correctly, in my view – as evil personified, and was prosecuted for his trouble. It seemed unlikely.

I understand why the police had to act the way they did. If a volunteer comes back and goes berserk in a supermarket they are the ones who will be vilified in the press for not doing something about the maniacs who have been out to God knows where doing God knows what. Fair enough. Of course it meant that I, and the others who went through the process, were not inclined to talk about anything of importance to those in authority until after the whole business had been dropped. As a result, any intelligence we may have had was old by the time it could be handed over or discussed.

I got off lighter than many. Five months on police bail, which meant I had to sleep at my parents' house and sign in once a week at a police station. Others I know have had to sign in several times a week for almost a year, making it difficult to find employment and even making it hard for some to retain lodgings.

Of course, there are long-term consequences to our arrests, even though no formal charge has, at the time of writing, been laid against any volunteer in this regard. It seems unlikely that I will ever be able to visit Australia or the United States again, and I think Canada and South Africa may also be awkward, from what I understand. Being arrested for terrorism leaves an indelible mark.

Oh well. No good deed goes unpunished, as they say. And the price I paid is much lower than many of the others. At least I came home.

On my last night in Rojava, at the foreigners' academy, I washed up after our evening meal. I had quite often done so in the time waiting to cross back into Iraq. Karatchok offered little but time to think, and I didn't particularly want to be thinking too much, so a chore was a welcome distraction. That evening one young volunteer offered to help me. He asked if I had any advice to pass on.

'Go home,' I told him.

He looked at me and said:

'Would you have just left if someone had told you to when you first came?'

I had to laugh. He had me there.

'All right. Get yourself good mates to back you up: foreigners, Kurds, Arabs, whatever. People you *know* you can rely on. Watch out for idiot orders, there's enough stupidity here to kill us all twice over. And don't do anything that you know is wrong. There'll be times when someone tells you to do something bad. Refuse. You're not a soldier, you don't have to follow orders blindly. You're a volunteer. You can tell them to go fuck themselves, quit and go home. Don't lose yourself for this fucking place.

'Finally, watch your arse. This place is fucking bad.'

The young volunteer's name was Ryan Lock. He died that December.

14

My Tac Mil

While writing this memoir I have worried that I have made too much of the failings of the YPG, the SDF and the political system that is being forged in northern Syria. It is easy to criticise failings, and no doubt there will be those who will in turn criticise this account. After all, who am I to comment on the military situation when I have no prior formal military experience and no real dedication to the political ideology at the heart of developments in the region?

There can be no doubt that war is a filthy business. When you are facing an enemy like ISIS, it's going to be even worse. With no regard for niceties like the protection of civilians or prisoners of war, they give you the choice of discarding your concerns and writing off the inevitable casualties inflicted on innocents, or else refusing to play that game.

Many people have asked me if I have any issues with what I did while in Syria. I can categorically say no. I chose to go, and those we fought against had also made their choice; things like the right to rape their captives and the deliberate targeting of children as a method of warfare. As these are anathema to me, I have no guilt or regrets about going to fight people who believe in such a hateful ideology or, quite frankly, in killing them. If people find that shocking, they haven't understood the nature of ISIS. I suspect events that have followed, such as the Manchester Arena bombing in May 2017, which killed twenty-two, many of them children, have demonstrated all too clearly the sort of thinking, and the lengths that they are willing to go to, of Islamic extremists. My sympathies are reserved for the victims of the crimes such people commit. For the perpetrators I feel nothing but contempt.

People always seem surprised by my lack of remorse and that I have not been affected by what I saw or experienced. To be honest, I am surprised at their surprise. I suspect the image we receive in the West of the troubled combat veteran and the psychological trauma that war inflicts colours our view, and as such the fact that I can be quite open about what I did and saw, and am unaffected (as far as I can tell), confuses people. In truth, while combat trauma and PTSD are very real conditions that should be properly treated in those afflicted, I have found that the reaction among most veterans to the assumptions of people who haven't seen combat mirrors my own; they find the automatic belief that they should be suffering psychological damage quite irritating and tiresome.

Another question I often face is was there any point to my going, did I achieve anything? Perhaps not on a grand scale, but I do believe that my presence, and that of my fellow volunteers, was appreciated by many of the people of Rojava, civilians and fighters both. On one occasion I was invited, along with my squad commander and two YPJ snipers, to have a meal with the family of one of my Kurdish colleagues. As home visits are a rare occasion for members of the militia, her entire family had gathered to see her and made us very welcome. My presence, understandably, caused some comment.

'Who is this man?' asked my colleague's grandfather, the patriarch of the family.

'This is Botan. He is one of the snipers in our tabor.'

'He is not Syrian! Where is he from?'

'He is from England.'

The old man's eyes opened wide in amazement.

'Why has he come here?'

I shocked him by replying myself, in my terrible Kurdish.

'I come to fight for you. Daesh is evil, dirty. They must be finished.'

'Many foreigners have come to fight for us, men and women. Many of them have died,' my squad commander told him.

The old man seemed genuinely astounded.

'They come to fight for us!?'

He jumped to his feet and came over to me, grasping my hands and, with tears in his eyes, kissed me on both cheeks.

'Thank you,' he said.

This was one episode of many among the civilian population in the country, and I know that most of my fellows had similar experiences. Do I think it was worth going? Yes. We let people facing terrible evil know that they were not alone. Wars are not won solely on the battlefield, and though the civilian population may have heard about the military assistance and the victories at the front, these things were remote to them. To see a foreigner walking down the road or even sitting drinking chai in your house, wearing the uniform of those fighting to protect you, is something that makes you appreciate that the world has not forgotten you.

I think back on my time in Syria, and especially with the YPG and SDF, with mixed emotions. Certain elements of the organisation anger me greatly. The blind belief in their own superiority, perpetuated by their propaganda machine, was directly responsible for many needless deaths among the soldiers who fought for it. In fact, the veneration of the Şehid, the martyrs, encouraged this attitude. A healthy society needs to remember and mourn their dead, and learn from their example. It shouldn't aspire to join them.

Another cause for concern was the extremity of certain elements of the ideology. Replacing extremist religion with extremist politics is not a solution, it's perpetuation by other means, different sides of the same coin and a recipe for further oppression.

But against this I must set the friendships I forged and the respect I have for the Kurds, Arabs, Assyrians and Turks that I met who fought against a great evil. Their determination to succeed, to build a better world, truly was inspiring. I sincerely hope that they achieve their goal. I believe that the society developing in Rojava and the areas liberated have great potential as a breeding ground for a new, more humane society if it is given the chance to flourish. I used to joke that I would take the YPG/SDF's nineteenth-century ideas over the opposition's seventh-century thinking. If other revolutionary movements failed as they fell to dictatorship and oppression, I hope that this one will be flexible enough, with enough inputs, to produce something viable and worthy of those who gave their lives.

And those lives should always be remembered. Because when ISIS arose, it was these people, of many races, creeds, religions and beliefs, who came together to oppose it.

Many of these were, and remain, close friends, and no doubt if you have reached this point in the book you wish to know what happened to some of the people I fought alongside.

My Kurdish squad commander, for whom I have the greatest respect and affection, eventually became the sniper tabor commander, something only his resistance to the idea had prevented for too long. The last I heard, he had been promoted beyond this and is expected to go far, a great example of promotion through merit that the YPG aspires to.

Del Gesh – the Canadian veteran I spent so much time with guarding the Euphrates, and who had to put up with my mockery after crashing his Hummer in the face of that first car bomb outside Al Hawl, as well as coming within a whisker of being blown to pieces by a later one – fought through the Tishrun dam campaign and then left Syria, returning to his homeland after various adventures I leave him to tell.

Roza saw it through to the end of the Manbij campaign, briefly went home to Sweden and then returned to continue fighting. She finally left after the fall of Raqqa in October 2017, having spent over two years in Syria. She still contacts me periodically to ask what we are doing next.

Akif, the ex-Marine, returned to the States, where he runs a security company. Ever the professional, Akif has been bodyguard to a number of celebrities and I have no doubt that a man of his drive and intelligence will do well. Mind you, he can't be that smart, as at the time of writing he has Kemal as a flatmate.

Inbred got over his beating at the hands of his supposed squad mates in no time: in typical fashion, he was back in the fight within days. Towards the end of the battle for Manbij he was hit by shrapnel from an RPG during a street fight and had to be evacuated to Kobane for hospital treatment. The campaign was over by the time he was fit to return and so, wisely deciding he had done his share, he went back to America. Now well and truly itching to see more of the world, he moved to Mexico and works in California. For all my mocking of Kemal, he's extremely smart; it certainly never occurred to me that you could live cheaply south of the border and commute. Like Roza, he occasionally drops me a line to see what's on the cards and what I am up to.

Larry went back to Sweden, and works on civilian projects aimed at helping the people in Syria with reconstruction and improving the situation in areas of the country where there is peace.

Moe and Curly both got plenty of aggravation from their respective governments after their return, which went on for well over a year, but at the time of writing we all stay in touch and meet up on odd occasions when we all happen to be in the same place. Curly's leg healed, despite him spending a month in a filthy KDP cell in Iraq, and he is once again one of the fittest people I know. Annoyingly.

Where we go from here remains to be seen, but I feel privileged to call them my friends, as they are all great examples of people who set out to try to help others at great risk to themselves.

Though there is plenty of criticism in this book of some of the attitudes and methods I encountered in my time there, I cannot but think that what I witnessed in northern Syria may actually be the best hope for an enduring peace, not just in Rojava, but perhaps as a pattern for the whole of the Middle East. The turmoil of the Arab Spring continues and we all wait to see what its result will be. I will watch, but I suspect that now my part has been played.

Early in 2017, military intelligence came to visit me. We spent more than three hours talking about what I had done in Syria and my observations on the conflict. One theme that came up several times was whether or not I would be going back again.

I didn't need to go back. As I wrote this book Russia and the coalition bombed Daesh into the ground, and the SDF took Raqqa in October 2017. American Marines had artillery in the country and no doubt used it to good effect. The US Army had Apache helicopters flying from the airstrip they built outside Hasakah. Much as I would have loved to see such firepower in use against an enemy I despised, there is little that I, one solitary sniper, could have added. Though I suspect the world hasn't heard the end of this repulsive ideology, the so-called caliphate is finished. Good riddance.

What there are, however, are tens, hundreds of thousands of people, perhaps even millions, all around the world who are suffering from conflict being waged by unjust men. You are unlikely to hear about them; they don't get a lot of attention in the media, wars that don't directly impact us and our comfortable lives. It is always this way, has always been this way and I suspect will always be this way. The unvoiced will continue to suffer, in myriad squabbles over control, power and wealth.

That's where I will go.

That's where I belong.

Changing Events

It shows how fluid the situation is concerning Syria that since my completing writing in early 2017 and publication in 2018 so many things have changed as to make some of my conclusions obsolete. Instead, the reader is best advised to consider the events of this book a snapshot of the situation as it stood in 2015 and 2016, and my musings as a product of those events.

The intervention of Turkey in the war and their invasion of Afrin has radically changed the dynamic of the conflict. It now looks as though the YPG may well face extinction and a resurgent ISIS, though perhaps under other aliases, will become a reality. I would hope that the outside world will finally attempt some real effort to halt the conflict, force those outside players whose presence continues the war for their own means to withdraw and allow the people of Syria their deserved peace. Unfortunately, I am extremely pessimistic about that possibility and it seems that so much suffering and bloodshed is doomed to have been wasted. Instead, it looks to continue unabated.

Also changed is the legal situation that British volunteers

face; prosecutions have started of some individuals under the Terrorism Act. As such actions seem to be motivated by political considerations rather than legal ones, it is possible I will face such charges myself at some point. So be it. I leave the reader to decide for themselves as to whether we deserve to be called terrorists or not.

Ed Nash
May 2018

Acknowledgements

As I am endeavouring to stay as low-profile as I can after writing a book, those I wish to thank for all the love and support I've been privileged to receive throughout my life will also mainly remain nameless – which will keep this short and sweet. But I do want to express my gratitude to my family and friends (you all know who you are) for putting up with the nonsense I make you endure occasionally.

To Adrian Searle of Wild Harbour Books, a more capable agent I doubt I could find and thank you for all the hard work you've put into this project. Don't take this to mean you can ask for a bigger percentage.

To the team at Little, Brown Book Group who have worked so hard to bring my ramblings up to snuff, I also offer unreserved thanks: Richard Beswick, who accepted the initial manuscript; Zoe Gullen, who has had to conduct dozens of rereads and cleaned the text up immeasurably; and Hayley Camis, who gets the unenviable job of trying to get me to play nice in public.

Of course, I need to thank Moe, Curly and Larry, mainly

because I'll never hear the end of it if I don't. Thanks for watching my back and keeping things interesting, even if you're all still laughing at me for falling down that bloody slope.

Thanks also to Kemal, Akif, Roza, Big Çudi, Angry Çudi, Welat, Josh and Danny (whose Kurdish names now elude me), Soro, Shervan Ameriki and the lads in 223, and the hevals of the sniper tabor. Again, you know who you are, and it was a privilege to know you all.

To Ryan, Jac, Big Jake, Dean, Martin, Jordan, Bill and John – rest easy. I'm proud to have known you all.